EXAM *Revision* NOTES

OCR AS/A-LEVEL
Critical Thinking

Jill Swale

Philip Allan Updates, an imprint of Hodder Education, an Hachette UK company, Market Place, Deddington, Oxfordshire OX15 0SE

Orders

Bookpoint Ltd, 130 Milton Park, Abingdon, Oxfordshire OX14 4SB
tel: 01235 827720
fax: 01235 400454
e-mail: uk.orders@bookpoint.co.uk

Lines are open 9.00 a.m.–5.00 p.m., Monday to Saturday, with a 24-hour message answering service. You can also order through the Philip Allan Updates website: www.philipallan.co.uk

© Philip Allan Updates 2009
ISBN   978-0-340-94618-3

First printed 2009
Impression number   5 4 3 2 1
Year   2014   2013   2012   2011   2010   2009

All website addresses in this book are correct at the time of going to press but may subsequently change.

Crown copyright material is reproduced with the permission of the Controller of HMSO (PSI licence number C2007001851).

Printed in Spain

Environmental information

Hachette Livre UK's policy is to use papers that are natural, renewable and recyclable products and made from wood grown in sustainable forests. The logging and manufacturing processes are expected to conform to the environmental regulations of the country of origin.

P01334

Contents

Unit 3 Ethical reasoning and decision making

Unit 4 Critical reasoning

Introduction

Critical thinking is a useful and fascinating subject to study as it enables you to evaluate arguments and evidence in other academic subjects, in the media and in everyday life.

Studying critical thinking at AS should help you to decide whether people are telling the whole truth or presenting a biased or incomplete picture. You will be provided with the tools for analysing and evaluating claims, inferences, arguments and explanations in a logical manner and will learn to identify a variety of flaws in arguments as well as being able to recognise the strengths of arguments and evidence. You should be able to judge the relevance and significance of information in a range of contexts and write short coherent arguments.

At A2, you will study ethical reasoning. This will enable you to identify moral dilemmas and make well-reasoned judgements and decisions by considering appropriate criteria and a variety of ethical positions. By the end of the course you should be able to write long, carefully structured, clear and convincing arguments of your own, as well as having acquired a better understanding of the world as a result of analysing passages about controversial and current issues.

The OCR examinations

This book has been written primarily for students following the new AS /A-level Critical Thinking specifications introduced in 2008. In order to do well in the course, it is important to focus on the three key assessment objectives, which are tested by OCR at both AS and A2:

- analyse parts of a passage containing an argument and identify its components (AO1)
- evaluate parts of an argument, identifying weaknesses and strengths (AO2)
- write your own arguments in response to documents and organise the information clearly and coherently (AO3)

In addition to reading this book, you should also work through plenty of examination papers so that you are aware of the types of questions set, what their wording means and the length and standard of answers that are required to obtain high marks. This entails handing work in regularly for your teacher to mark or, if studying independently, comparing your answers with the mark schemes on the OCR website (**www.ocr.org.uk**). If you are taking AS exams in 2009 or A2 exams in 2010, there will be no actual examination papers for these new specifications to work from, but there are specimen papers and you will find practice papers modelled closely on them, for example in the Philip Allan Updates workbooks and teacher resource packs written for this specification.

Practise shorter exercises using the Philip Allan Updates workbooks and similar resources and read as much advice as you can from experts, for example by looking at the examiners' reports on previous similar papers on the OCR website. Units 2, 3 and 4 from the previous specification are similar enough in many ways to provide some useful practice, but bear in mind that there have been significant changes, for example in the length and quality of arguments of your own required by Unit 2.

Timing can be a problem in critical thinking examinations, so ensure that you make several attempts at papers for each unit in timed conditions. If you realise that you rarely finish them in time, seek advice about whether your answers are unnecessarily long. If not, you may need to omit a few low-mark questions in the paper, returning to them after tackling the high-mark questions if you have time.

This all sounds like hard work, but critical thinking can be amusing and fun, as you begin to notice the flaws in arguments made by people around you. If you apply your emerging skills to real-life situations, especially the media messages that bombard us every day, you should start to enjoy the subject and appreciate the new insights it has provided.

How to use this book

For each unit covered in this book, you will find explanations of vocabulary and concepts, together with examples set in appropriate contexts to aid your understanding. In addition, there are questions to think about and worked examples, sometimes illustrating different levels of achievement. You will find out the criteria examiners use to judge your answers and there are tips on how to earn the highest marks.

At the end of each unit is a revision checklist. This is intended as a quick reference as your examination approaches. Read through it and if there are aspects that you cannot remember or find tricky, refer back to them again. The key terms index at the back of the book should help you to locate definitions and examples for particular terms.

If particular areas continue to cause difficulty, read more about them in your textbook or class notes. Then return to this revision book to consolidate your understanding and work through past papers testing the appropriate skill or practice papers based on the specimen one. Make yourself notes, either linear ones or mind maps, depending on your preferred learning style.

The revision checklist is short enough for you to look over just before your examination to remind yourself of the relevant terminology, such as the credibility criteria and names of flaws.

Critical thinking is not just about passing examinations. Apply it to your other studies and use the tools in everyday life when you encounter advertising material, hear a political debate or participate in a discussion with your family and friends.

Tips for success in critical thinking

- Ensure that you work through lots of examination papers, answering the questions in writing. Look carefully at the number of marks for each question as a guide to how much to write. Timing is crucial. Work out how much time to spend on each section and stick to it.
- If you expect to have timing problems, consider tackling high-mark questions first.
- Seek feedback from your teacher about how to improve your marks.
- Look carefully at mark schemes from OCR.
- Look at the examiners' reports on past papers on the OCR website. These discuss errors candidates made in particular questions and provide useful tips.

- Practise so that your analysis of the structure of arguments is sound. This tends to be students' least favourite area but carries a significant number of marks in Units 1, 2 and 4.
- Make sure you are fresh and alert for the examinations.
- Read a variety of textbooks about critical thinking and browse through the numerous websites about it on the internet.
- Most of all, take an interest in the world around you. Controversies in the news, documentaries about current issues, radio programmes such as *The Moral Maze* and *Any Questions* and challenging discussions with friends will make you aware of a wide range of opinions that you can use in arguments of your own. Noticing the flaws and strengths in other people's arguments will soon become second nature to you and make you aware of the benefits and relevance of critical thinking.

1 Introduction to critical thinking

A The language of reasoning

1 Analysis

The first few questions of the Unit 1 examination are likely to ask you to analyse the structure of an argument by identifying various **components** or **elements**. This means that you need to understand and memorise vocabulary which has to be used with precision.

1.1 Identifying an argument

An **argument** is a written or spoken attempt to convince or persuade, using **reasons** to support the **conclusion**. In critical thinking expressions of opinion not backed up by evidence are not called arguments.

Reason(s) plus conclusion = argument.

Here is an example:

> As rail travel is less damaging to the environment than air travel, tourists should be encouraged to take trains instead of planes.

The first part is the reason and the last part is the conclusion. The word 'should' indicates that the writer is trying to convince the reader.

Despite its name, a conclusion does not necessarily come at the end of an argument. Consider this example:

> Tourists should be encouraged to take trains instead of planes because rail travel is less damaging to the environment than air travel.

In both cases, the conclusion is the same, 'Tourists should be encouraged to take trains instead of planes', but in the first example it follows the reason, whereas in the second it precedes it.

Because reasons and conclusions can appear in any order in an argument, students sometimes find it difficult to distinguish them. However, there are often verbal clues, known as **indicators**, that help you to identify them.

Conclusions are often preceded by the **conclusion indicators** *therefore, so, consequently, hence* or *thus*. They may include words such as *must, should, need* or *ought to* if they are recommending some course of action.

Reasons are often preceded by **reason indicators** such as *because, for, as* and *since*.

Sometimes you have to work out from the context which parts of the argument consist of reasons and which part is the conclusion that can be drawn from them, regardless of the order in which they are presented on the page. Here is an example:

> Critical thinking must be a good test of intelligence. Our students' grades relate closely to their IQ scores.

The second sentence is clearly the reason that supports the conclusion stated in the first sentence.

If there is no indicator word, it can be helpful to mentally supply two alternatives to see which one best fits the sense. This may help you identify the conclusion. Try the conclusion indicator word *so* and the reason indicator word *because* between the two sentences above.

> Critical thinking must be a good test of intelligence **because** our students' grades relate closely to their IQ scores.

Clearly *because* fits well, whereas *so* would make no sense, confirming that the second sentence is the reason and the first is the conclusion. Another approach is to consider the order of the reasoning process involved. In this scenario, noticing the correlation between the two sets of results would lead to the conclusion that critical thinking is a good test of intelligence, not the other way round.

Arguments can be supported by one or more reasons. Look at this example:

> Universities prefer students to study more than three AS subjects (R1) so you should add critical thinking to your other choices (C). The skills will be particularly helpful if you intend to do LNAT, UKCAT or BMAT tests (R2).

In this case there are two reasons given for studying critical thinking, one preceding the conclusion and one following it. Notice the use of the **notations** (abbreviations) for the **components** (elements or parts) of the argument, R1, R2 and C, which the examination board encourages you to use.

Sometimes people state something they believe without giving a reason. Such a statement is called an **assertion** or a **claim**. It may be an attempt to persuade or an expression of opinion such as:

> Cabbage is good for you.

or:

> George Bush was a successful president.

Though both of these present conclusions, they are weakened by the lack of supporting reasons or evidence.

Another use of the word **claim** is when witnesses make statements about what they have seen or done or about their innocence or someone else's guilt. They make **claims** in court or when interviewed by the media. An example is:

> I saw the soldiers shoot indiscriminately into the crowd.

In Section B of the Unit 1 paper, you will be asked to identify the claims made by particular individuals in a document and to assess their credibility. Some may be unsubstantiated by other witnesses.

Explanations are also different from arguments. Although they have reasons and conclusions, they are not attempting to persuade. They may provide evidence to support statements that are already accepted as facts by public consensus, for example:

> You will need to alter your watch when you go to France because of the time difference of 1 hour.

In the passages you are likely to encounter in critical thinking examinations, explanations sometimes set the scene or clarify a situation, increasing the reader's knowledge and understanding. They may then be followed by an argument.

Biofuels are any kind of fuel made from living things, or from the waste they produce. In recent years, the term has come to mean ethanol and diesel, made from crops including corn, sugarcane and rapeseed. Burning the fuels releases carbon dioxide; but growing the plants absorbs a comparable amount of the gas from the atmosphere.

However, we should be much more wary of assuming that using biofuels is a solution to global warming. Much energy is expended in farming and processing the crops. Cutting down rainforests to make way for palm oil plantations increases rather than decreases carbon emissions.

In the above example, the first paragraph offers an explanation about what biofuels are and why they have become popular. Providing this type of background material is also called **scene setting**. The second paragraph expresses an opinion indicated by the word *should* in the conclusion:

we should be much more wary of assuming that using biofuels is a solution to global warming.

The following two sentences provide a reason and an example supporting the conclusion. It is more likely that you will encounter examples of scene setting and other components accompanying arguments in Unit 4 than in Unit 1, but from the beginning of the course it is important for you to be able to identify an argument and recognise its structure.

1.2 Counter-claims and counter-arguments

Most of the material in an argument tends to consist of reasons, evidence and examples supporting the main conclusion, but often there may be reference to opposing views, which are then dismissed. A brief contrary statement which is introduced without its backing reasons is called a **counter-assertion** or **counter-claim**. For example, an argument against biofuels might begin as follows:

Many people think biofuels are the answer to the environmental crisis, but they are sadly mistaken.

The words before the comma state the counter-claim (CC), which is immediately challenged. This **challenge** or **response to the counter-claim** (RCC) is likely to be followed by reasons why relying on biofuels is mistaken.

A **counter-argument** would usually be longer than a counter-claim, providing one or more **reasons** why many people think biofuels are the answer to the crisis. Each reason might then be dismissed in turn to support the main conclusion of the argument.

See if you can identify the counter-argument (CA) in the passage that follows.

The government should think twice about attempting to increase the amount of time devoted to sports at school. Forcing reluctant teenagers to participate in outdoor team games in freezing weather can put them off sport for life. Defenders of school sports argue that the exercise counteracts obesity and strengthens the bones of the young, reducing the likelihood of osteoporosis in later life. However, encouraging youngsters to walk to school every day would be of more benefit on both these counts than the amount of physical activity a reluctant student is likely to participate in on the sports field. Improved education about diet could also do more to build healthy bodies than compulsory sport.

You should have worked out that the first sentence is the main conclusion, and this is supported by the reason in the second. The third sentence, about defenders of school sports, is the counter-argument and it is supported by reasoning about two benefits of sport. The next sentence is a **response to the counter-argument**, undermining its reasoning, signalled by the word *however*. The argument is completed by another reason supporting the main conclusion.

1.3 Distinguishing reasons from evidence and examples

In the arguments we have examined so far the main conclusions have only been supported by one or two reasons. The conclusions of longer arguments are usually drawn from a number of reasons, most of which may be supported by **evidence** (Ev) and **examples** (Ex).

If asked to identify the reasons upon which the conclusion is based, make sure you look for these main points rather than being distracted by the details that support them. Think of the reasoning involved as a series of steps or levels in a hierarchy:
- Reasons are the general points saying why the conclusion is true.
- Evidence often consists of research findings, statistics and the opinions of experts which substantiate a reason.
- Examples are specific instances illustrating a more general point.

Analyse the passage below to identify the conclusion, reasons and evidence.

> Fathers should be permitted to stay overnight in post-natal wards and medical staff should involve them more in the care of their newborn babies. A man's sense of responsibility for his child tends to be weakened if he feels excluded straight after the birth. According to the Fatherhood Institute, maternity hospitals frequently emphasise the mother's responsibility for the newborn baby but give the father the impression that he is not needed in the hospital. Fathers also need information about caring for babies, which they could easily learn from the hospital staff. In a MORI survey for Mothercare, only 3% of males correctly answered four basic questions about looking after newborn babies.'

Hopefully you identified the first sentence as the conclusion. The two reasons supporting it are the following broad points:

> A man's sense of responsibility for his child tends to be weakened if he feels excluded straight after the birth.

> Fathers also need information about caring for babies, which they could easily learn from the hospital staff.

The sentences that follow each of these reasons are supporting evidence, in each case from a well-informed source. If the passage had contained a specific instance of a father who had felt excluded after his baby's birth, this would have been an example. It may help you to distinguish evidence from reasons if you think about how you would create a briefer version of the argument. You would exclude the evidence but not the reasons or conclusion.

1.4 Hypothetical reasoning

Reasons are always put forward as being true, but on examination may prove to be unconvincing. Occasionally you may encounter the word **premise** instead of **reason**. Its meaning is virtually the same: a proposition or piece of evidence the arguer believes to be true on which an argument is based or from which a conclusion is drawn. The role of the critical thinker is to examine reasons and evidence carefully to see whether they are really strong enough to support the conclusion.

Arguments can be supported by reasons based on everyday observations, generally accepted facts, the results of research, statistical data, eyewitness testimonies, opinions of the arguer or experts, hypothetical reasoning or by general principles.

Hypothetical reasoning is often based on what is likely to arise from possible future conditions. This type of reasoning, frequently signalled by the indicator words *if* and *then*, can be challenged on the grounds that there is no certainty about what will happen in the future. Part of the above passage could be rewritten as follows:

> If new fathers are allowed to stay with the mothers and babies in maternity hospitals, then they will take more responsibility for their children in the long term.

Though this seems likely, it is really only conjecturing about a future possibility. If the practice became common, some men might still take little responsibility for their own children. The argument is weak because we cannot predict the future with any certainty.

An even less convincing type of hypothetical reasoning is about the past, supposing what would have happened if events had been different, for example:

> If the atomic bomb had not been invented, fewer people would have died in the Second World War.

This argument is flawed because if one past event had been different then so might many others. The war might have lasted for longer or some other weapon of mass destruction might have been invented instead. Past events are already established facts so speculating about how they could have turned out differently cannot be based on any evidence and is therefore profitless, however interesting it may be.

In the examination you may be asked to identify hypothetical reasoning as part of the analysis of components of the argument, in which case you should particularly look out for speculations about the future, even if the actual words *if* and *then* do not appear, for example:

> The government is intending to prolong compulsory education and training to the age of 18. Should this happen, British workers will be better qualified to compete with foreigners seeking work here.

Remember simply to copy out any component you are asked to identify. You may lose marks if you attempt to paraphrase it or write out a briefer version of it.

Alternatively in assessing the quality of the argument in part of the passage, you might quote an example of hypothetical reasoning as a weakness and explain why.

1.5 General principles

These are statements about the values or rules that should govern the workings of an organisation or guide people's behaviour. They are called general principles because they are expected to apply not just to a single situation but universally. Two examples are:

> Adults should always put children's needs before their own.

> We must seek to preserve the natural world.

Sometimes principles are implied or assumed rather than explicitly stated. In Unit 1 you should be able to pick out a principle as a component of the argument, but you are more likely to encounter questions evaluating them in the Unit 2 paper.

1.6 Assumptions

An assumption is an unstated part of the argument; something which is taken for granted and not mentioned directly because it seems obvious to the arguer. Sometimes it is called a **supposition** instead. There are no indicator words preceding assumptions because they are not explicit, so they may be relatively difficult to spot. Here is an example:

> My student son is coming home for the Easter holidays (R). He will be disappointed unless I make time to go out and buy him a big Easter egg. (C)

What are the assumptions needed to make this argument work? There are several including:

> My son still adores chocolate.

> My son has not reduced his previous consumption of chocolate for health reasons.

> He will not already have been overwhelmed with Easter eggs from other people.

> Going out to buy Easter eggs is preferable to ordering them online.

The first assumption is probably the most obvious.

In this argument, there is only one stated reason for the conclusion but the assumptions perform a similar function, playing an invisible but still significant role in a chain of reasoning that could be written out as follows:

> My student son is coming home for the Easter holidays (R1). He still adores chocolate (R2) and has not reduced his previous consumption of chocolate for health reasons (R3).

> He will not already have been overwhelmed with Easter eggs from other people (R4).

> He will be disappointed unless I make time to go out and buy him a big Easter egg (C).

> Going out to buy Easter eggs is preferable to ordering them online (R5).

One way of being certain that you have correctly identified an assumption is to apply the **reverse** or **negative test**. By changing the assumption to its opposite (e.g. 'My son no longer enjoys chocolate') you should find that the conclusion can no longer be reached.

Analysis questions may simply ask you what the author has to assume for the argument to work, in which case you would compose a statement such as one of the above. Remember that *nothing which is written in the document can possibly be an assumption*. In everyday language people sometimes use the word 'assumption' for a statement which the speaker thinks is true but others disagree about, for example:

> Men are better at map-reading than women.

You might want to query it by protesting, 'That is just an assumption!' However, in critical thinking such a broad and unsubstantiated claim would be called a **hasty** or **sweeping generalisation**. Assumptions are essential but **invisible parts of a chain of reasoning**. Because they occur so often, it is likely that you will be asked to discuss their reasonableness as well as simply identifying them, demonstrating your skills of evaluation.

1.7 Tips for analysing arguments

When asked to identify components or elements of arguments, you should quote the author's exact words rather than producing a paraphrase or summary. Usually 2 or 3

marks are awarded for accurate quotation and fewer marks if you write it in your own words. Unlike in other subjects, when analysing argument structure you should not write in your own words to demonstrate understanding of the material.

If the conclusion stated in the passage was:

> The government should do all in its power to discourage smoking.

and you wrote:

> Smoking should be strongly discouraged.

you would be likely to lose at least 1 mark, as you have omitted the reference to the government.

> Smoking should be discouraged.

is even further from the original, as it is less emphatic, and might only earn 1 mark out of 3.

> Smoking should be banned.

is so different in meaning from the original that your answer would be unlikely to be rewarded.

So take the easy way and copy out the relevant phrase or sentence. *Remember that critical thinking requires great precision of expression.*

An exception to exact copying is if the quoted phrase has a pronoun in it. Replace words such as 'it' or 'they' with the appropriate noun to make complete sense of the statement. Words which indicate the direction of the argument such as 'however' and 'moreover' may also be omitted if quoting components such as counter-argument or reasons.

Ensure that you do not quote more than the component required. If asked to quote the reason in a particular paragraph, exclude any examples and evidence embedded within it. For example, in an argument warning against the dangers of illegal drugs, one of the reasons for banning them might be presented in the text as follows:

> Many illegal drugs, such as cannabis, are believed to affect the memory.

You would need to write out:

> Many illegal drugs are believed to affect the memory.

as the rest of the sentence is an example.

Ensure that you do not confuse evidence with reasons. Generally speaking, each paragraph is likely to contain a reason supported by some evidence or examples. The reason is likely to be a broad point and the evidence more illustrative and detailed. Anything that mentions specific people, places or statistics is likely to be evidence.

Many students find highlighters or pencil underlining a useful way of identifying the main components of arguments. Different colours can be used for different components, or you can use them to underline any flaws in reasoning you notice as you first read the passage.

As an alternative to questions asking you to identify the components of a passage, a particular sentence or phrase from it may be quoted and you will be required to name the component and explain its purpose in the argument. This means you need to be able to define components concisely and be able to explain how they relate to other elements of an argument.

2 | *Evaluation*

Part of Section A of Unit 1 requires you to judge whether arguments, reasoning and evidence are strong or weak, giving reasons for your assessment and explaining in appropriate language using technical terms where appropriate. This will include identifying flaws in reasoning, such as unjustified assumptions, and explaining why the reasoning may be weak. (Detailed knowledge of more flaws in reasoning is required for Unit 2.)

2.1 Assessing assumptions

As well as identifying an assumption the writer must make to support the reasoning in a particular passage, you may be required to assess whether it is a **reasonable** assumption to make, referring to the material in the passage.

This will involve examining the type of assumption being made. Does it assume some factual point and, if so, how easy would it be to access the relevant evidence? The example below is of this type:

> Girls are doing so much better than boys in school subjects that soon all the best jobs will be taken by females.

Here the assumption being made is:

> There is a high correlation between school qualifications and level of employment subsequently obtained.

The passage may contain information confirming or contradicting this, but if not, evidence of this type could be established by researching the qualifications of employees of a representative sample of establishments. You could write that the soundness of this assumption could be checked but that the information was not presented in the passage.

Alternatively the assumption might be based on an opinion. Here is an example:

> Girls are doing so much better than boys in school subjects that soon employers will have to positively discriminate in favour of male employees.

An assumption here, in addition to the one above, is that:

> Males are too important to be outnumbered in the job market by females.

Clearly this is a biased opinion. You could take a cautious approach and write that the reasonableness of this assumption is not easy to establish because it is a matter of judgement, not fact. A stronger response might be that the assumption is unjustified because it is subjective.

A slightly different approach could be to identify the assumption as an unstated **principle**:

> Equal access to the job market for both sexes is desirable (regardless of qualifications).

Some principles are established by wide consensus, but all moral principles are a matter of opinion, not fact. You could briefly discuss how widely held such a principle is likely to be and say that, if there is likely to be any disagreement, the assumption is unjustified.

Sometimes assumptions are based on speculations about future events and both the above statements fall into this category. They assume that because girls are doing better than boys in school now, they will continue to do so. The assumptions could be rephrased as **hypothetical reasoning**, based on the *if…then…* structure.

> **If** girls are doing well academically now, **then** they will continue to do well in the future, (affecting the gender balance of the job market).

As we can never predict the future with certainty, assumptions based on hypothetical reasoning should be assessed as unsafe. Nevertheless the passage may provide some idea of the probability of the predicted events occurring and thus it might be possible to estimate the extent to which the assumption might be a reasonable one to make.

To sum up, assumptions may be assessed as **reasonable** or fairly **sound, safe** or **justified**. Alternatively they may be blatantly **false** or **unjustified**, or it may be necessary to defer judgement by pointing out the nature of the assumption and whether it would be possible to establish its reasonableness by research.

2.2 Evaluating claims and reasons

As suggested above, claims may be based on 'hard evidence', opinion, principles, hypothetical reasoning, everyday experience, gossip, reasonable or unreasonable assumptions, and they should be assessed accordingly.

Reasons must provide sufficient support for the conclusion and so they need to be adequate.

> Cars should be banned because some people drive them dangerously, causing harm to others

is an inadequately supported argument. The folly of 'some people' is insufficient grounds for banning the majority from an activity, unless the harm done vastly outweighs the benefits, which has not been suggested here. At best, the reason supplied gives only **limited support** to the argument. The conclusion is **overdrawn**: too sweeping for the evidence. A different conclusion for which the reason might be seen as adequate is:

> People convicted of driving dangerously on several occasions pose a severe risk to the public so they should be banned from driving.

Adequate means that words in the conclusion such as *no, ever, always, everyone, definitely*, or the implication that this claim can be applied **universally**, are justified by the reason given. In this case it would not be justifiable to ban all drivers, but it would be justifiable to ban all those frequently convicted of dangerous driving.

The **significance of evidence** is a similar concept. Evidence may be relevant and valid yet not sufficient to carry the argument because of other factors. Consider this example:

> Sociology attracts far fewer students than psychology at our college. We should drop the sociology option for future years.

How significant the relatively low uptake for sociology would be in this scenario could depend on a number of factors. In a large well-funded college, where 200 students opted for psychology and 50 for sociology, the sociology course could still be described as popular and economically viable. In a small school on a tight budget, a class of three sociologists might be considered less sustainable. Even then, an argument might be made for preserving a minority subject in the interests of allowing students wider choice. Popularity might be viewed as less significant than meeting individual needs. Significance then relates to the adequacy and importance of evidence relative to other factors that might lead to a different conclusion.

Evidence must also be **relevant**. Look at the following example:

> Children should not be asked to take home classroom pets to look after in the school holidays. Rabies is a life-threatening disease.

Assuming that the argument relates to British schools, it is highly unlikely that classroom pets would suffer from rabies. This would normally only be the case if they had recently been introduced illegally from abroad, a risk a responsible teacher would not take. It is more likely that the irrelevant reason results from the arguer's ignorance of UK law.

Another aspect of poor reasoning is **selectivity** of evidence.

> Don't take your holidays in Brittany. Tripe sausages are their speciality.

is an example of **selective evidence**. Though andouillette is served throughout Brittany, there are many alternative dishes, and the cuisine is only one of many factors to consider when choosing a holiday. The arguer has produced a misleading impression by focusing on only one.

Of course some reasons are simply based on incorrect facts or are so irrationally argued and contrary to common sense as not to be **reasonable**. Evidence may not be **plausible** or **credible** (believable) because the witnesses involved are not **reliable** (trustworthy and unmotivated to lie). Close examination of the degree to which witnesses can be believed is the subject of Section B of Unit 1.

2.3 Evaluating evidence

Many of the arguments you are likely to encounter in critical thinking documents, as well as in your other academic studies, will be based on evidence from research. In the examination you may be asked to evaluate the strengths or weaknesses of such evidence. Some of the aspects you should consider are outlined below.

Sample size

If only a small number of people were consulted about their experiences or views, this will not present enough data upon which to base conclusions. Likewise evidence from a single institution, such as the results from one school, will not be sufficient to produce a generalisation.

Representativeness of sample

A sample might be very large yet still not reflect the views of people from many different backgrounds. To choose a **representative sample**, the researcher has to decide what attributes of potential interviewees would be likely to impact on their experience or opinions about the topic in question. These are often age, gender, social class and

ethnicity but other factors might be more crucial in particular circumstances. In a survey of A-level students, the subjects they studied and whether they were members of year 12 or year 13 might be considered significant influences on their likely responses.

Once a detailed picture is obtained of the whole target population, the researcher should then choose a representative sample of respondents reflecting all these different subgroups in the **correct proportions**. Using volunteers, personal acquaintances (an opportunity sample) or people in the street is unlikely to generate a representative sample.

Be wary of research conducted by particular media organisations on their own readers or viewers. Views collected from *Daily Mirror* readers or Radio 4 listeners are unlikely to reflect the full range of attitudes you could expect from a national poll reaching all social groups.

How and when the evidence was collected

It is important to check that any research data being used to support a conclusion is **recent** and **relevant** to the location, types of people and situation being discussed in the argument. Research into alcoholism in Glasgow might not necessarily be transferable enough to suggest ways of tackling the problem south of the border.

Sociologists and psychologists try to collect their data in carefully controlled conditions, seeking privacy for their interviewees and ensuring that they understand the questions. However, amateur researchers may try to interview people with others listening, making them less likely to tell the truth, or they may stop people in the street who have little time to answer properly and lack interest in the subject. To be **valid**, data have to reflect a true picture of the situation being studied. This means that the respondent must fully understand the questions, take them seriously and be motivated to tell the truth.

In the examination, you should examine the source of any research data provided and attempt to make a reasoned judgement about how professional the body conducting it is likely to be.

Ambiguity of findings

Research results are sometimes interpreted in a way that fits the expectation of the researcher. For example, when girls were less successful in A-levels than boys, one of the reasons suggested was that little girls tended to play with dolls while boys ran around outside. It was thought that, because dolls resembled babies, girls' horizons were narrowed so that they viewed motherhood rather than academic excellence as their natural sphere. Physical play outside was thought to encourage boys to be more assertive, adventurous and therefore more successful in competitive spheres such as education.

However, now girls have overtaken boys in A-level success, some sociologists interpret the same patterns of play in entirely different ways. Girls are said to learn effective communication by role-playing with dolls, and the sedentary nature of such play prepares them for the discipline of the classroom. Boys' outdoor play provides little practice in verbalising ideas and is poor training for sitting still and concentrating in a classroom.

Which of these contrasting explanations is correct? Is playing with dolls better or worse for educational success than physical play outside? The example demonstrates that the connection between a piece of evidence and a conclusion is not necessarily clear cut.

Data apparently supporting one conclusion can potentially be interpreted in a different way to support a contrasting one. This may be particularly the case when data are qualitative (based on impressions conveyed through words) rather than quantitative (figures based on the precise measurement or counting of phenomena). Nevertheless statistics are by no means completely reliable.

Alternative interpretations of statistics

Researchers rarely publish all the raw statistics they have collected, preferring to process them so readers can understand the general trends. The **mode** is the most common score in a series; for example, in a test more students scored 11 out of 20 than any other number. However, the **mean** (average) mark could be considerably higher or lower if the majority of students scored a lot more or less than 11. The **median** mark (the middle score of all of them) would probably be different again. Instead of using these measures of central tendency, an alternative way of representing the scores would be by the **range**, for example from 4 to 20, but this would give us no idea at all of how any but two of the students had fared. Anyone wishing to present the efforts of the class in a particularly positive or negative way might present their scores in the way most likely to produce the required impression and researchers may do the same.

Likewise journalists and others, such as advertisers, using persuasive language in public may select particular statistics to support their argument, ignoring other available data which might have conveyed a different or more balanced impression. Members of the political party in power are well known for citing figures for decreases in certain types of crime while ignoring increases in other types, while the opposition is likely to do the opposite. Phrases such as 'up to three quarters' can be very misleading, since this is so vague it could refer to a very low proportion.

In the case of data based on interview questions, it is worth enquiring exactly what was asked. The finding that only 3% of people who were asked where they would like to go on holiday chose France might give a very negative impression of the country's tourist potential, but if you knew that respondents were only allowed to select three options from a list of 50 countries, the result would be less surprising.

2.4 Tips for evaluating arguments and evidence

- Ensure that your answer is thorough enough. The space in the answer booklet suggests the length of response required. The number of marks is another indication. For example, if you were asked to identify a strength of the evidence in a particular paragraph and you wrote, 'the sample size is large', this might only merit 1 mark because it is not fully explained. You would be more likely to score the 2 marks available if you wrote: 'The sample size is large, which increases the chance of a wide variety of views being represented.'
- Make sure your response is as carefully worded as possible. Mark schemes insist that answers should be well expressed and detailed for full marks.
- Read each question twice to ensure that you have grasped the meaning. Examiners only reward relevant answers.
- Questions worth 5 or 6 marks need some planning. These may ask you whether the reasoning in a whole paragraph supports the writer's overall argument. In such a case there could be two or more points to make, perhaps relating to the relevance or adequacy of the evidence given, the methods used to obtain it or the relevance of

the examples. There could be 10–12 ruled lines in the answer book, indicating how much you are expected to write. Your response should be paragraphed, expressing your points in accurate technical language illustrated by references to the text. Your spelling, grammar and punctuation need to be good.

B Credibility

In this part of the examination you will encounter one or more documents presenting different points of view about a particular scenario or different accounts of an event. In other words, the people or organisations quoted will be making contrasting claims. You will be required to identify and assess the different claims, for example by considering their credibility and the evidence which supports or undermines them. This may include making an assessment of whether visual material, such as photographs or graphs, really supports the claims it accompanies. Occasionally a claim will strike you as **implausible** (highly unconvincing), regardless of what is known of the person making it, simply because it is contrary to commonsense and experience. This is a valid type of evaluation.

However, most of your judgements will be reached by applying **credibility criteria**, the names and meanings of which you must learn as they will not be provided on the examination paper. A criterion is a standard, rule, or test on which a judgement or decision can be based; the plural form is criteria.

1 *Credibility criteria*

1.1 Circumstances or context

This refers to details of the actual situation in which the event took place or the claim was made. Examples include weather conditions, time of day or year, locality or clues at the site that could help people infer what might have happened. Skid marks on a road, footprints and fingerprints are circumstantial evidence. By applying this criterion it might appear more likely that illegal drug-taking had occurred if the location was a student party rather than a pensioners' club in a church hall.

1.2 Reputation

This may relate to facts about the character of particular individuals mentioned in the text, such as a police record or involvement in previous accidents. If no such information is provided, it is legitimate to conjecture how reputable those making claims may be on the basis of their professions or similar attributes, even though this sounds rather stereo-typical. For example, British clergy, doctors, police and members of the legal profession are expected to be honest and we would expect most of them to be able to give accurate accounts of events. Professionals, intellectuals and business leaders have to consider their public reputations so it would be unwise for them to lie.

The differing reputations of media sources should also be considered. The BBC, quality national newspapers such as *The Times* and *Guardian*, and government websites are generally viewed as more reliable than popular and local media and amateur sources of information such as personal websites.

1.3 Ability to see or perceive

Consider whether **eyewitnesses** were able to see well, bearing in mind factors such as distance from the event, weather conditions, distractions, obstacles and time of day. CCTV evidence may be indistinct and photographs may have been manipulated, as may sound recordings.

When assessing media evidence, consider whether the reporter was present at the scene and was therefore an eyewitness or **primary source**. If not, was the information simply bought from a news agency, a **secondary source**, or from an interviewee closely involved in the incident? Did the interviewee see events at first hand or hear about them from others, depending merely on **hearsay**?

1.4 Vested interest

Consider what a witness or interviewee would personally gain by making a false, biased or selective claim. By winning a court case a person might gain compensation, whereas the unsuccessful party might risk a penalty and loss of reputation. This could be a powerful incentive to present a distorted account of events. In the case of media sources, concerns about national security, election success or attracting more readers may influence the slant of a story. On the other hand, some people may have a vested interest in presenting an accurate and unbiased account. If their responses are likely to be publicised, their future careers may be jeopardised if they are shown to be manipulating the situation for their own advantage or reporting carelessly about an area relating to their profession.

1.5 Expertise or experience

Think about whether witnesses or interviewees have relevant knowledge and experience to give sound evidence. They may be too young or not know enough about the specific field in question. Sometimes there may be an overlap between expertise, reputation and vested interest where the media source, organisation or professional in question is highly skilled, has an excellent reputation and wants to maintain it. In such a case, select whichever criterion strikes you as most appropriate or apply more than one, so long as each is explained separately in the relevant context.

1.6 Neutrality

Lack of neutrality means that a witness or claimant is likely to favour a particular position or party because of emotional ties. **Objectivity** is lost because of friendships, family relationships, nationality, religion and other affiliations. Witnesses are more likely to be neutral if they know none of the people involved in the incident.

In the case of a newspaper or website, consider whether it has right- or left-wing **bias**, which country it is written in or what other interests it may reflect. Neutral sources are likely to include evidence and views from conflicting sides and the BBC always tries to do this, even though some people argue that it has a moderate agenda, avoiding interviewing extremists of all types.

Do not confuse lack of neutrality with vested interests. People lacking neutrality may not tell the whole truth because of fellow feeling for others involved in the issue. Those with vested interests might lie for personal gain or to avoid some harm to themselves.

2 Applying the credibility criteria

You are likely to be asked to assess the credibility of particular individuals, organisations or media accounts by identifying, applying and explaining appropriate criteria. When doing so it is wise to:

- Name each criterion you are applying using the key terms given here, not phrases of your own. For example, write '(lack of) ability to see' in preference to 'poor vision'.
- Explain how the criterion is relevant in the context; for example, making it clear why the witness might not have been able to see well as he was a long way from the incident.
- Use the phrase 'weakens credibility' or 'strengthens credibility' and be explicit about whether the criterion makes the claimant more or less believable.

You will usually be asked to make two or three points. Unless the question specifically asks for different criteria, it can be acceptable to use the same criterion twice about the same claimant, both to weaken and to strengthen their credibility if it seems appropriate. For example, you might want to argue that a motorist was directly involved in an accident so had the ability to see, strengthening his credibility as an eyewitness. However, his very involvement may have caused him to panic, affecting his ability to see and recall accurately what was going on, reducing his credibility. Nevertheless, it is wiser to choose different criteria if you can, to show the examiner the breadth of your knowledge.

3 Assessment of visual material

Some of the documents you encounter in the Unit 1 examination may be accompanied by photographs, graphs or artist impressions of events. There are likely to be questions asking you to assess the degree to which these images or their accompanying captions support the claims being made.

You may be asked to explain whether a graph or chart is relevant to the discussion in part of the document, in which case you may need to scrutinise verbal material such as captions, what is being measured and dates as well as the impression gained by the data within the figure itself.

Ask yourself the following questions about photographs or images you have to assess:

- Could the photograph have been faked, manipulated or cropped to suggest an event that did not really happen or to create a misleading impression? For example, it is very easy nowadays to enhance the beauty of models by making their legs look longer.
- Look at the background of a photograph to see if it enables you to judge the scale of the crucial objects.
- How certain can you be that this photograph is a typical example of what is being described and not a 'worst case scenario' or a site specially cleaned up for the photograph?

- Is the photograph too blurred or small for you to be certain what is being shown? For example, it may be a CCTV image taken in poor light which makes it difficult to be sure about the identity of the person concerned.
- Could the camera angle or lighting be contrived to make the people or situation look particularly threatening? For example, photographs taken from below speakers or in front of oncoming marchers or police can make their looming shapes quite alarming. Close-ups of speaker's mouths, wagging fists or pointing fingers, or of animal's teeth rarely create a favourable impression.
- Does the object that has been photographed look like the genuine article or could it be a model or a toy replica?
- Was the artist who created an impression of the scene likely to have been present at the time or could the drawing be a reconstruction, perhaps based on facts supplied by a biased party?
- Scrutinise the captions accompanying illustrations. In newspapers there is a tendency for the caption to convey a simpler message than the article itself. Though this may be for reasons of brevity, it is nevertheless misleading and therefore worthy of mention in your assessment.
- Does the accompanying caption convey exactly what is shown in the photograph and relate precisely to the claims in the passage or are there minor but significant differences between them?

4 *Tackling other types of questions*

Other types of questions you are likely to encounter in the credibility task are discussed below.

> What else would you need to know in order to reach a judgement about the credibility of a particular claim?

The answer here will obviously depend on what important information is missing from the document, but some possibilities are that we would need to know:

- whether the person making the claim represents the views of many or is expressing only a personal opinion
- whether the person making the claim was present throughout the incident referred to or is relying on someone else's account of it (ability to see)
- whether the person making the claim is likely to be rewarded in some way, for example by his or her employers, for making the claim (vested interest)
- whether the person making the claim is an expert in the specific field in question as opposed to the general area associated with his or her profession (relevant expertise)
- whether the person making the claim has close relationships with those whose views or interest his or her claim is supporting (lack of neutrality)

Your answer would need to be detailed enough to match the number of marks available, clarifying the possible effects on the person's credibility if these facts were known.

A variation on this question, requiring the negative equivalent of the answers above, might ask what you would need to assume in order to believe the person's claim.

Identify a piece of evidence that supports or conflicts with a specified claim.

This should be simply a matter of accurately copying out evidence that is consistent or inconsistent with the person's statement. The word 'identify' does not imply the need for an explanation. Do not reword the evidence any more than necessary or you may lose marks for inaccuracy.

Identify one or more claims that support a given statement.

Copy out the claims accurately, saying who made them and naming the document if there is more than one.

Assess the reasonableness of a particular claim, with reference to material from the passage.

This type of question is likely to carry more marks than the identification questions, perhaps about 4. It may require the same type of evaluation skills as in Section A. You may need to consider the nature of the claim, whether it is based on apparently 'hard evidence', opinion, hypothetical reasoning, experience or hearsay. Judge any evidence given according to whether it is adequate, significant, relevant or plausible enough to support the reasons expressed. Consider whether the evidence or opinions expressed are internally consistent or are in conflict with other material in the passage.

Make an informed judgement about which of two claimants is the more credible, making two developed points that contrast their relative credibility.

This may be the final question on the paper and may carry more marks than previous questions, perhaps about 6. It needs careful planning, as simply repeating what you have already written about the claimants will not attract marks. You may argue for either of the people or sources being the more credible so long as this is consistent with the rest of your answer. The key word is 'contrast'. You need to weigh up the weaknesses and strengths of each person's credibility and balance them against each other. This could include **corroboration** (confirmation) from other sources if you have space, but there may only be time to use some of the CRAVEN criteria (circumstantial evidence, reputation, ability to see, vested interest, expertise and neutrality).

As the claimants are likely to have different points in their favour, it is important to suggest which two of the criteria you consider to be the most important and decisive in this particular scenario, providing a convincing reason why. You might, for example, compare the claimants from the point of view of expertise, clarifying the areas in which they have specialist experience and how relevant this is to the situation being discussed. Then you might point out that, despite a little more expertise, one of the individuals has much greater vested interest in lying, explaining why. This is a particularly significant point because this individual's testimony is in conflict with another witness. The second individual has, in contrast, no motivation to lie, and so it can be concluded that he or she is the more credible.

Answers worth this many marks are assigned to levels by the examiners according to particular criteria. They then decide on the exact mark within the band according to how thoroughly the requirements are accomplished. The descriptors for a top-level answer, worth 5–6 marks, for a question of this type in the specimen paper read as follows:

Criteria for top-level marks
- A well-expressed and relevant response that compares/contrasts the credibility of the two people, showing which of the factors is the more important in making a judgement.
- Two detailed points are made.
- Grammar, spelling and punctuation are good.

> Make a reasoned judgement about the probable course of events in a given scenario.

This question did not appear in the specimen paper but has been flagged up as a possibility in the course specification. 'Reasoned judgement' implies a well-organised, extended and balanced answer similar to the one above about relative credibility. The question is likely to arise from conflicting accounts of the same incident. It would therefore be necessary to consider what the various eyewitnesses and others said had occurred, and think about their relative credibility and any corroboration or conflict between their versions. Then summarise the most plausible course of events, commenting as you go on relevant claims and why you find them more believable than contrasting ones, referring to appropriate credibility criteria and details from the text.

> Suggest several reasons why particular contexts such as war, natural disaster or accident might affect the credibility of reports about the incident.

This question appeared frequently on credibility papers before 2008 and so it is wise to be prepared in case it appears again, though it is not given as an example on the specification.

Depending on the scenario, you could think about the possibilities outlined below.

Whether there could have been physical difficulties in perceiving what happened
- This could relate to the number of people present, such as too many or too few.
- Were those present likely to be paying attention or were they otherwise engaged?
- Was the situation orderly or chaotic?
- Would the conditions, such as time of day, weather and nearness to the event, make accurate observation possible?
- If some factors such as time of day are not mentioned, it may be useful to discuss what difference this might make. However, commonsense is needed. Unusual factors such as a heavy fog would be mentioned if they applied.
- These factors relate to the criteria of ability to perceive and circumstances.

Whether factions might have different motives for misrepresenting the truth
- This could include those who might be held responsible for an incident, directly or indirectly. Not only those present but their employers, supervisors or those maintaining the site, equipment or checking health and safety conditions could in some cases be held responsible.
- Victims, relatives or friends of injured parties may be looking for others to blame. They may be hoping for financial compensation.
- Pressure groups campaigning for change might want to use some aspect of the incident to draw attention to their cause.
- Sometimes national, political or professional interests are involved. Witnesses might tend to favour members of their own group.

- There might be security or confidentiality reasons for suppressing some information.
- These factors relate to the criteria of vested interest and lack of neutrality.

Difficulties of reaching a final judgement
- There may be no surviving witnesses or it might have been difficult for objective reporters to reach the scene in time to establish the facts.
- Those corroborating (supporting) the evidence of participants may have limited credibility for reasons of bias or inability to see well.
- The evidence on either side might be similarly strong or weak, making it difficult to reach a judgement.

5 Final tips for Unit 1

- Ensure you memorise definitions of components and terms for assessing evidence such as 'adequate' and 'relevant' so that you do not confuse them.
- Learn the credibility criteria, ensuring that you do not confuse vested interest with lack of neutrality.
- Quote carefully when asked to identify components, claims or evidence from a passage.
- Answer in the appropriate amount of detail to fit the marks available, explaining your answer where necessary.
- Practise working in timed conditions.
- If time is short, concentrate on the questions carrying the most marks, usually those at the end of the section or paper.

C Revision checklist for Unit 1

1 The examination

OCR codes
- AS Critical Thinking subject code: H052
- Unit 1 code: F501

Mark allocation
75 marks, 50% of the total AS GCE marks. In the specimen paper, Section A was worth 35 marks and Section B was worth 40 marks.

Timing
1 hour 30 minutes. The advice in the OCR specification is to spend about half an hour of the examination time on Section A and about 45 minutes on Section B. This leaves some time for checking.

Practicalities
Write answers for both sections in black ink in the spaces provided on question paper.
The examination consists of two sections:
- Section A: The language of reasoning
- Section B: Credibility

2 Section A: The language of reasoning

This primarily tests your skills of analysis (AO1) and evaluation (AO2) though quality of communication (AO3) is always assessed.

2.1 Analysis

You should be able to identify an argument (as opposed to an explanation, claim or assertion, for example) and to recognise that it has a structure with reasons and a conclusion linked together. Being able to recognise argument indicators will help with this analysis. The early questions on the paper are likely to ask you to identify the following components or elements in the reasoning of the passage provided:

- main conclusion
- reasons in particular paragraphs
- counter-assertions or counter-claims
- counter-arguments
- evidence
- examples
- simple hypothetical reasoning, which takes the common 'if this, then that' form
- assumptions, including instances where an argument requires more than one assumption and instances where an assumption may also be a general principle

When asked to identify such components you should quote the author's words rather than producing a paraphrase or summary.

Alternatively, a particular sentence or phrase from the passage may be quoted and you will be required to identify what component it is (e.g. a counter-assertion) and perhaps also explain its purpose in the argument.

2.2 Evaluation

You will be required to assess the claims made in the passage provided, by commenting on:

- the type of reasoning involved; for example, whether it is hypothetical or based on sound evidence
- the size of any survey sample quoted
- the representative nature of the sample
- how and when the evidence was collected
- the potential ambiguity of any findings
- alternative interpretations of any statistics

In addition:

- you will need to judge whether the reasons or evidence offer adequate or only limited support for the claims being made
- you should be able to identify assumptions in a particular paragraph and to assess their reasonableness
- you are likely to be asked to identify strengths and/or weaknesses in the reasoning, explaining why it does or does not support the conclusion
- You may be asked to supply a reason that would support a particular argument

As well as the above short questions, which are likely to earn between 1 and 3 marks each, you may have to write a longer answer assessing whether the reasoning in a particular paragraph supports the author's overall conclusion. This might occupy 10–12 lines of your answer book and be worth about 6 marks. For this task, good planning, organisation and expression are essential.

3   *Section B: Credibility*

Section B primarily tests your skills of evaluation (AO2) though in order to assess the material you will need to recognise any components of argument, such as assumptions, mentioned in the questions (AO1). Quality of communication (AO3) is always assessed.

You should be able to identify and assess different claims in the source material, for example by considering the plausibility (credibility) of the claim and the evidence that supports or undermines it and giving reasons why it may or may not be plausible.

In the context of a simple scenario, you should be able to identify and apply appropriate criteria for judging the credibility of individuals or sources referred to in the document and sometimes of the document as a whole. You should be able to explain how claims are strengthened or weakened by the following criteria:
- circumstantial evidence or aspects of the context: 'hard evidence' such as traces of an activity found afterwards may support a particular claim; certain contexts may make it easier or harder to believe in the accuracy of a particular version of events
- reputation, positive or negative, which could come from past performance and behaviour or commonly held opinions of certain professions or sources
- ability to see or perceive, including an understanding of the relative reliability of primary sources (eyewitness testimony) compared to secondary sources, and a consideration of factors that could distract, disorientate or confuse an observer
- vested interest, when there could be a clear gain from telling or misrepresenting the truth
- expertise or experience of sources or witnesses
- neutrality, when a balanced account is given or when a person has no known connection to parties involved in the scenario

Use the mnemonic CRAVEN to remember the above. In addition consider the following:
- general plausibility or reasonableness of claims or evidence
- bias in situations where a one-sided account is given or when a person's background or experience disposes him or her to a particular viewpoint
- corroboration of witness accounts
- consistency within a witness account
- inconsistency or conflict between different accounts or claims

You should also be able to:
- identify and explain what other information would be needed in order to reach a judgement about the credibility of a particular document or source
- compare and contrast the relative credibility of individuals or documentary evidence within a given scenario, by selecting and applying appropriate criteria (this is likely to entail a well-organised passage of assessment worth about 6 marks)
- make informed judgements about the most or least credible source within a scenario
- make a reasoned judgement about the probable course of events in a given scenario

A Analysis of argument

In addition to the components or elements of argument covered in Unit 1, in Section A of the Unit 4 paper you need to be able to recognise the following and be able to explain their role in the structure of the argument in the passage provided.

1 *Intermediate conclusion*

While a short argument may consist only of a couple of reasons supporting a single conclusion, longer arguments often consist of groups of reasons supported by evidence and examples. Each of these leads to a preliminary conclusion, known as an **intermediate conclusion**. This may be the case when you write an essay. Each paragraph or section may end with a sentence such as 'This shows that' or may begin with a general statement which is then supported by the rest of the paragraph. These concluding or opening sentences may be intermediate conclusions. The main, final or overall conclusion of your essay, which is likely to be in last paragraph, is supported by these intermediate conclusions.

In the hierarchy of a complex argument you could say that intermediate conclusions function both as conclusions to groups of reasons and the evidence supporting them and as reasons supporting the main conclusion.

A useful definition to learn is as follows:

> An intermediate conclusion is a conclusion drawn on the way to the main conclusion, supported by reasons, but acting itself as a reason for the main conclusion or other intermediate conclusions.

Even in a relatively short argument, you may find an intermediate conclusion preceding the final one. Consider this very brief argument:

> You have a massive file of notes, so it will take you a long time to read through them all and digest the content.

Here the first seven words provide the reason for the conclusion which comes at the end of the sentence. The conclusion is highlighted by the presence of the conclusion indicator word 'so'.

However the role of the words at the end of the sentence changes if we add more:

> You have a massive file of notes, so it will take you a long time to read through them all and digest the content. You need to begin your revision early.

Now the second sentence is the main conclusion (C). The component 'so it will take you a long time to read through them all and digest the content' forms a step in the line of reasoning between the reason (R) 'You have a massive file of notes' and the main conclusion. It has become an intermediate conclusion (IC), as it is a conclusion drawn on the way to the main conclusion.

In Section A of the Unit 2 paper, it is important to be able to distinguish intermediate conclusions from conclusions. Several of the multiple-choice questions may ask you to identify either an intermediate conclusion or a main conclusion from a range of options.

A Analysis of argument

Some of the distracters (wrong options) for a conclusion question are likely to be intermediate conclusions and vice versa.

Likewise you will need to be able to distinguish the two in the longer passage on the document accompanying Section B and C questions. Remember that the order of an argument on the page does not necessarily reflect the order of the reasoning. Just as a conclusion may precede a reason in a very short argument, a conclusion may precede an intermediate conclusion. It is quite common in a long passage for the conclusion to be the first sentence and the intermediate conclusion to be the last. If you cannot decide which one is the main conclusion, try the 'therefore' test. Say both statements with 'therefore' or 'so' in between them and then reverse them and do it again. This will help you to decide which follows logically from the other.

As this is so important, here are two passages to analyse. In each case, try to identify the main and intermediate conclusions and the other components such as reasons, evidence and examples.

Argument 1

People who are very similar tend to be attracted to each other. However, when we know someone is a relative our strong incest taboo normally makes us resist any attraction to him or her. It is therefore important that people know who their close relatives are. Occasionally siblings are brought up apart without knowing who their biological parents are, as in the recent case of the twins parted at birth who married each other and later found out their true identities. People who adopt children must ensure that they are informed about their biological parents as early as possible.

Argument 2

Health-conscious people should try to reduce the amount of processed meats that they eat or cut them out altogether. Recent research has raised a health alert about these types of food. Professor Martin Wiseman, the World Cancer Research Fund's medical and scientific adviser, said 'We are more sure now than ever before that eating processed meat increases your risk of bowel cancer. Whether you are talking about bacon, pastrami or ham, the safest amount to eat is none at all.' Clearly people who eat processed meat regularly are putting their health at risk.

Cancer is a major cause of death in Britain today. One in 20 people develops bowel cancer and 16,000 people die from it each year. Many cancers are related to aspects of unhealthy lifestyles such as diet, so it is possible for people to reduce the likelihood of being affected by the disease.

The answers are as follows.

Argument 1

People who are very similar tend to be attracted to each other (R1).

However, when we know someone is a relative, our strong incest taboo normally makes us resist any attraction to him or her (R2).

It is therefore important that people know who their close relatives are (IC).

Occasionally siblings are brought up apart without knowing who their biological parents are (R3),

as in the recent case of the twins parted at birth who married each other and later found out their true identities (Ex).

People who adopt children must ensure that they are informed about their biological parents as early as possible (C).

This argument is quite straightforward in order. The first two reasons lead to a preliminary conclusion which constitutes the third sentence. The third reason introduces a specific situation with an example and, building on the support of the intermediate conclusion, leads to the final conclusion.

The second argument is more complex and less obvious in its structure as there are two strands of argument, each leading to an intermediate conclusion. The first strand is about the dangers of eating processed meat and the second is about how people can reduce the chance of cancer affected by lifestyle. These two intermediate conclusions lead logically to the final conclusion that combines these two ideas.

Argument 2

Health-conscious people should try to reduce the amount of processed meats that they eat or cut them out altogether (C). Recent research has raised a health alert about these types of food (R1). Professor Martin Wiseman, the World Cancer Research Fund's medical and scientific adviser, said 'We are more sure now than ever before that eating processed meat increases your risk of bowel cancer. Whether you are talking about bacon, pastrami or ham, the safest amount to eat is none at all' (Ev and Ex). Clearly people who eat processed meat regularly are putting their health at risk (IC1).

Cancer is a major cause of death in Britain today (R2). One in 20 people develops bowel cancer and 16,000 people die from it each year (Ev). Many cancers are related to aspects of unhealthy lifestyles such as diet (R3), so it is possible for people to reduce the likelihood of being affected by the disease (IC2).

2 *Analogy*

An **analogy** is a comparison used as part of the reasoning in an argument. The writer may try to persuade you that the situation in question is similar to a less controversial one. It is argued that what is almost certainly true for a familiar situation must therefore be true for the apparently similar issue in question. Here is an example:

> The Yorkshire Ripper is making a legal bid for freedom by claiming his human rights have been breached. Peter Sutcliffe, who was jailed in 1981 for murdering 13 women, will argue that the Home Office disregarded his human rights because it failed to fix a tariff for his sentence. Harry Smelt, whose wife, Olive, survived an attack by Sutcliffe, said 'He didn't give the victims many human rights, did he?'

(Extract from *Metro*, 15 May 2008)

In the above passage, the conclusion to Harry Smelt's argument is implied rather than stated, but it is clear that he is making an analogy between Sutcliffe's treatment of his victims and how the criminal justice system should treat him. His suggestion seems to be that, as the Ripper accorded his victims few human rights, he should receive few and therefore should not be freed.

The questions you encounter about analogies are likely to require both analysis and assessment. You may be:

- asked to identify the component in a particular paragraph by copying it out
- told there is an analogy in a particular paragraph and asked what is being compared
- asked how well the analogy supports the author's argument (or asked to assess its effectiveness, which means the same)

(This last type of question requires evaluation skills, which are discussed on pages 35–49.)

Explaining what is being compared in an analogy requires some precision and candidates may lose marks by responses that are too brief or vague. In the example above, stating that the Ripper was being compared with his victims might not be a thorough enough answer to earn full marks. It is more precise to say that the Ripper's entitlement to human rights is being compared to his victims' human rights entitlement.

3 *General principles*

General principles are 'rule-like' statements or guidelines about behaviour that is not limited to a specific situation. Principles sometimes act as reasons to support arguments, though they can be found in other contexts, such as the mission statements of organisations.

Many such principles are moral principles, making universal statements about how people should or should not behave or what our values or priorities should be. As such they are expressions of opinion rather than claims about which absolutely everyone would agree. In some contexts, principles are underlying assumptions in an argument rather than being explicitly stated.

In the Unit 2 exam, you could be asked to:
● identify the best statement of a general principle being used in a short passage from a series of options in the multiple-choice section
● identify the general principle in a longer passage as a Section B question
● evaluate how consistently the principle is applied, whether it conflicts with other principles, reasons or evidence within the argument or possibly how reasonable it is

In Section C of Unit 2 you could be asked to:
● construct an argument on a given topic including a principle as a reason
● construct an argument on a given topic supporting or challenging a principle supplied

A phrase reflecting current UK government policy is 'Every child matters'. This could be rephrased as the general principle 'We must prioritise the needs of children'.

During the recent debate about the abolition of the 10% income tax band, there was an outcry from members of the government who thought low earners would suffer relative to high earners. The protesters were supporting the principle that 'We should consider the needs of poorer members of society' or 'The prosperous should not be allowed to benefit at the expense of the poor'.

Notice that principles are quite broad. 'We should try to offset the abolition of the 10% tax band to help the poor' is not a principle because it only applies to one specific situation. Principles usually begin with phrases such as

> We should…
>
> Society must…
>
> People ought not to…
>
> It is wrong to…

or make use of a passive construction such as

> The needs of X must be given priority.

Examine the letter written by two readers to the *Guardian* below and answer the questions that follow. To help you understand the comment, 'internment' means imprisonment without trial, a situation in which the state makes no formal charges against which prisoners can defend themselves. This relates to the imprisonment of terrorist suspects while evidence is sought against them.

> It's always been our understanding that in a liberal democracy the role of the police was to protect our freedoms. When did those hard-won principles become inverted so that the overriding concern becomes disproportionate police powers — i.e. proposals to introduce internment? When did the terrorists win?
>
> (Extract from the *Guardian*, 27 July 2007, **www.guardian.co.uk**)

1 Identify the principle the letter writers associate with a liberal democracy and why they think it has been 'inverted'.

2 Suggest how a counter-argument could reason that internment is upholding one of the principles of a liberal democracy.

In answer to question 1 you might identify the principle as 'The police should protect public freedoms' or 'A democracy should prioritise people's civil rights'. You would not include a reference to imprisonment without trial as this would be too specific.

In your explanation, however, you would explain that upholding this principle entails fair treatment by the criminal justice system. This appears to be undermined by imprisoning suspects indefinitely without charge because insufficient evidence is available. (For your interest, it contravenes habeas corpus, the traditional right to be charged with a named offence so that it is possible to organise a defence and have a fair trial.)

In answer to question 2 you could suggest that a counter-argument might reason that by taking those suspected of trying to harm the public off the streets, the police are upholding one of the principles of a liberal democracy. This is that the law-abiding majority should be free to go about their own business in safety.

4 *Distinguishing explanations from arguments*

How these differ has already been discussed in Unit 1 (see page 6). In Unit 2 you are expected to be able to distinguish between them. Remember that an argument must be attempting to persuade, to change behaviour, beliefs or attitudes as opposed to simply informing. An argument must have reasons and a conclusion, and the conclusion must follow from the reasons. A collection of pieces of evidence or reasons together with a conclusion that is not clearly connected is not an argument. Look at the following options and decide which one is an argument.

(1) The washing machine is making a bleeping sound so that indicates that it will be safe to open it.

(2) Research suggests boys are reluctant readers whereas most girls enjoy it. They also have shorter attention spans than girls. The sexes need to be taught in different ways.

(3) Gerbils are small rodents which originally come from desert areas. There are about 110 different species. You should definitely choose gerbils as pets for your children.

(4) AS levels were developed in 2000, partly to provide qualifications for students who started life in the sixth form but then decided to terminate their studies after one year. In addition studying more than three subjects provides a broader academic experience than formerly.

The only proper argument is the second passage because it provides two reasons supporting a conclusion that is intended to persuade. Other people could provide reasons why the sexes should be taught together, such as social ones. There is no conclusion indicator but the word 'therefore' is implicit.

Sentence (1) is an explanation of how the washing machine functions. The presence of the conclusion indicator 'so' makes it clear that reasoning is taking place, but not necessarily persuasion.

The third passage is not an argument even though there is a persuasive conclusion. The first two sentences are not reasons supporting the conclusion. They consist of an explanation of what gerbils are and an additional rather random fact.

The fourth passage is also an explanation. It offers two reasons why AS levels were adopted but there is no conclusion and no attempt to persuade. This could be made into an argument if an opinion-based conclusion were added such as 'Therefore the AS system is a great improvement on the previous system'.

5 Key terminology

You should be able to understand and use the following terms accurately, according to their meaning in critical thinking.

5.1 Counter

As a verb, this means to oppose an argument, usually by providing reasoning against it. It is used as a prefix in words such as 'counter-argument', 'counter-assertion', 'counter-claim' and '**counter-example**' (one which suggests an exception to evidence amassed to support the main argument).

5.2 Challenge

As a verb, this means the same as to counter an argument. Section C of the Unit 2 paper will ask you to write an argument either supporting (giving reasons and evidence in line with) or challenging the main conclusion in the document. Challenge is also used as a noun. A counter-argument or counter-claim is often followed by a challenge, also known as a response to the counter-argument, for example:

> Although some people think A-levels have become easier over the years (counter-claim), they are mistaken (challenge or response to the counter-claim). Examinations have in fact become much harder (conclusion). This is because… (reasons and evidence would follow)

5.3 Assess

This synonym for 'evaluate' usually invites you to consider an example of reasoning and identify strengths **and/or** weaknesses, supported by explanation and, if appropriate, quotation. In such a case, make a conscious effort to consider strengths as the emphasis of your course may have been to focus much more on flaws.

5.4 Strength and weakness

At other times, questions may specifically direct you to identify and explain only strengths such as adequacy, relevance and large samples. Alternatively they may ask you to identify a number of weaknesses, to name the flaws and to explain why they are examples of poor reasoning.

5.5 Opinion, belief and knowledge

These familiar words are included in the list to enable you to distinguish between different types of evidence. An opinion is **subjective** (a personal view) and is therefore not as reliable as evidence as knowledge, which is universally accepted as **objective** (neutral or unbiased) fact. The word 'belief' carries the possibility of error. Many beliefs are shared by large numbers of people on the basis of substantial evidence, but others may be held by individuals on the basis of faith or complete misunderstandings. If a belief is stated, it can be called a claim.

5.6 Reasoning

This refers to a coherent and logical pattern of thought leading from one step to another, usually employing reasons, evidence, intermediate conclusions and other components, to reach a conclusion. As well as in arguments, reasoning is employed in explanations and in tentative academic explorations of ideas such as theories and hypotheses. The word is sometimes used in a looser way to refer to the way a writer has attempted to persuade in a long passage which may include emotional appeals and flaws; poor reasoning in fact.

5.7 Coherent

A coherent argument is a meaningful and well-reasoned one where the steps flow logically from each other and all points are relevant.

5.8 Consistent

A consistent argument is one without internal **contradictions**. All the evidence and reasoning **corroborates** or supports it.

5.9 Contradiction

Contradiction or **conflict** occurs when two or more claims undermine each other, showing that at least one cannot be completely true.

5.10 Converse

The converse of a statement is one where the key sections, such as subject and direct object, have been reversed. The converse of *Drug addiction increases unemployment* is *Unemployment increases drug addiction*.

Note that the word converse means 'the other way round', not 'the opposite' (which would be *Drug addiction does not lead to unemployment*).

5.11 Refute

Refute means to prove a claim wrong.

5.12 Repudiate

Repudiate means emphatically to reject an argument or idea. This could be by employing good reasoning or by offering poor reasoning or no reasoning at all, by **ranting**. This contrasts with refuting a claim, where the reasoning has definitely been successful in dismissing it.

5.13 Structure

The structure of the argument refers to its various components or elements and the order and way in which they function to support its conclusion.

5.14 Draw a conclusion

Multiple-choice questions will sometimes invite you to identify the best statement of the conclusion you would draw from a list of options relating to the evidence presented in a short passage. In such a case you would need to work through the evidence and examples and choose a conclusion which is broad enough to flow from all the evidence. Ensure that it represents the final stage in the reasoning and is therefore the overall conclusion, not an intermediate one.

5.15 Inference

An inference is something a reader, listener or observer infers or works out from the evidence or clues in a text, in the spoken word or similar stimulus. As the word is not used when the point being inferred is **explicitly** (directly and openly) made, there is always a chance that the reader may interpret the evidence wrongly, **inferring** something that is not true.

5.16 Implication

A word that is often confused with inference is **implication**. This refers to the indirect suggestion that something may be the case, as opposed to directly (**explicitly**) stating that it is. Remember that a passage or speaker **implies** or suggests something, whereas the reader or listener **infers** the **implicit** meaning.

It is quite common to find examination questions such as:

> What is the arguer inferring from the evidence he has quoted in paragraph 2? What alternative explanation could there be for the phenomenon he observed?

or:

> What could the passage imply is the reason for...?

5.17 Ambiguity

Ambiguous statements can be interpreted in different ways because of double or even multiple possible meanings.

Lexical ambiguity involves vocabulary with two or more meanings, as in the example,

> She gave the persistent tramp a couple of socks to make him go away.

The intended meaning could be clarified by rewriting the sentence as

> She gave the persistent tramp a couple of socks as his feet were bare.

or

> She gave the persistent tramp a couple of socks on the jaw and he staggered off in pain.

Referential ambiguity arises when it is unclear which of several possibilities is being referred to. Here is an example:

> Coursework can enable students to follow their own interests but occasionally they may plagiarise material from the internet or elsewhere. Some examination courses have consequently discussed withdrawing the coursework option, resulting in a vociferous teachers' protest. This is totally unacceptable.

In this case it is unclear whether the final sentence is expressing dismay at the teachers' protest or the possibility of withdrawing coursework, as the word 'this' could refer to either.

Examination questions may ask you to assess evidence, and this may sometimes be ambiguous. For example, '75% of NUT members expressed no wish to go on strike' could mean that:

- 75% of those balloted by the NUT voted NO to going on strike
- 75% of those balloted by the NUT either voted NO or abstained
- 75% of all NUT members did not express support for the strike, many of them did not participate in a ballot at all so their views are unknown

You should be able to see that the first option gives a much stronger impression of opposition to strike action than the other two.

Another type of question is the multiple-choice one asking you to select the closest definition of an ambiguous word or phrase as it is used in the passage. Read the paragraph below:

> Doubts about the good sense of the British justice system have recently been raised. Sarah Davies (20) was awarded a £75 fine for littering when she offered a small piece of sausage roll to her daughter in a park and the child dropped it on the ground. Gareth Corkhill was fined £210 for overfilling his wheelie bin so the lid was raised a few inches. When others receive only cautions for vandalism and theft, can this really be justice?

> (Facts from the *Daily Mail*, 25 April 2008)

Which of the following is the closest in meaning to the word 'justice' as used in the final sentence?

- the treatment of others in a fair and equitable manner
- the administration of law with the objectives of protecting victims and lawfully punishing perpetrators

It should be clear that the first definition is the most appropriate. In contrast, the second definition fits the word's use in the first sentence of the passage.

B Evaluating arguments

Brush up on your analysis of the strengths and weaknesses of types of evidence, including statistics, from Unit 1. In addition, learn the names of the following flaws, getting as much practice as possible in recognising them in context. Ensure that you are able to explain why they constitute poor reasoning.

1 Flaws

1.1 Slippery slope or thin end of the wedge

This is a misleading chain of argument. It usually involves describing a situation that is supposedly deteriorating or that will deteriorate in an alarming manner if the first stage is allowed to occur. The flaw lies in the fact that at one or more links in the chain, the arguer makes an imaginative leap that may not be justified. He or she predicts that something negative is bound to happen, when it might not, or that the trend will affect huge numbers of people, when it might only happen to a few. Here is an example.

> Students should avoid taking out a loan if they go to university. The loaned money gives them the false sense of being well off, tempting them to spend the full amount of each year's loan on unnecessary luxuries. Then at the end of the course when they are unable to get a job straight away, they have to start paying interest on the loan. As each year passes, the amount owed increases and so does the interest, making paying it off increasingly impossible. Mortgage lenders and others are reluctant to lend more money to the indebted, meaning ex-students can never have a home of their own. Discovering this breeds hopelessness, relationship break-up and depression, often leading to suicide.

It should be easy to see why this is a flawed argument at various stages. Not all students will use their loans so foolishly and some may find well-paid jobs swiftly and be able to repay the loans. Mortgage companies take loans into account but will sometimes lend to those whose earnings make it feasible for them to pay the loans off gradually. Not everyone would be deeply depressed by being unable to buy their own home.

1.2 Unjustified prediction

A variation of the slippery slope is the prediction based on limited information. Media sources often alarm the public by projecting current trends into the future. For example, a claim might be made that a rise in a particular type of crime or harmful activity, such as binge drinking over the past 5 years, might continue at an equally steep rate over the next few decades, eventually resulting in a huge epidemic. In reality it is likely that steps would be taken to curb the behaviour or that people in the future would find new ways of behaving badly! Remember that the phrase 'if trends continue' heralds a hypothetical argument based on guesswork only.

1.3 Post hoc argument

This Latin phrase means 'after this'. It refers to the assumption that if an event follows 'after this' it was caused by this. For example, if a school's examination results in critical thinking improved after a particular critical thinking teacher had left, enemies of that teacher might be keen to suggest a reason. However, it could be that results improved because the new specification was clearer or more recent cohorts of students happened to be more motivated.

1.4 Circular argument

This argument is one that appears at first to offer useful new information, but nothing new is really learnt or proved. This flaw in reasoning is also known as 'begging the question' because, despite appearances, it avoids the question rather than addressing it. Here is an example:

> Acts of crime and deviance occur most often in areas known as zones of transition. If you are trying to identify zones of transition in your town, you can easily recognise them by the high amounts of crime and deviance that occur there.

In this case, the first sentence appears to be about to offer an explanation of crime, but then the reader is let down by being offered a definition of zones of transition which simply loops back to the contents of the first sentence.

A more frequently cited example is when you are asked to accept a religious teaching because it is in some holy book. On querying the truth of the holy book, you are told to believe it because it is the words of a particular god or prophet. However, the only evidence for the existence of the god or prophet lies in the book itself.

1.5 False dichotomy or restricting the options

A dichotomy refers to two possibilities. This type of reasoning puts forward a limited number of possibilities, usually two, from which the listener is invited to choose. Sometimes one is made to seem particularly unattractive as the other is the option the arguer wishes the listener to choose. If the listener does not think clearly enough to realise other possibilities exist that have not been mentioned, he or she may be misled into choosing the least unattractive of those offered.

> Doctor to sick child: Would you like the injection in your arm or your bottom?
>
> Child: I'd rather not have it anywhere.

In this example, the precocious child has noticed that the options are restricted more than they need be.

A more cynical approach may be employed by advertisers:

> Do you want to risk your family facing disaster if your house is destroyed by flood or fire?
>
> Ask for details of our insurance policies today.

1.6 Conflation, arguing from one thing to another and unrelated conclusion

Conflation refers to confusion over terms, specifically referring to two slightly different concepts as if they were exactly the same, such as 'poverty' and 'deprivation' or 'intelligence' and 'ability'. The terms are blended together unjustifiably in the muddled thoughts of the arguer, or have been deliberately confused to mislead the reader. Look out for passages where evidence based on one of the concepts sounds quite convincing

and then this is supposedly backed up by evidence related to another slightly different concept. The conclusion is then presented, referring to only one of the concepts or perhaps to yet another concept not quite the same as either. This is poor reasoning because the evidence relating to some of the concepts was not as relevant as the argument implies. The conclusion reached is not supported by all the reasons and evidence.

It is easier to see this in practice. Consider what is wrong with the following argument:

> Comprehensive schools are widely supported because they are designed to give all students equal access to learning. Yet most of them are streamed. In order to ensure that all pupils have the same education, it is inappropriate to set them into different ability groups, so all comprehensives should reject the idea of streaming their students.

You should be able to see that the concepts of 'equal access to learning' and 'same education' are conflated. People agreeing that all local children of the appropriate age should be allowed equal access to the same local school would not necessarily expect them all to have the same lessons when they got there, regardless of their abilities and interests. The conclusion can only be reached if we accept that all pupils should have the 'same education' and this has not been established by the reasoning in the first sentence, even though careless reading might suggest that it has.

1.7 Problems with cause and effect

Many arguments rest on the assumption that if two factors are found to **correlate**, one has caused the other. (Correlation means different factors going up or down at the same rate over time — positive correlation — or one factor going up as the other goes down — negative correlation.)

For example, legislation about homosexual acts has been gradually liberalised since 1967 and at the same time the rate of teenage pregnancy has increased, yet it would be totally illogical to argue, for obvious reasons, that the increased pregnancies are due to greater homosexual activity.

Nevertheless you will find arguers using correlations as evidence that juvenile crime has increased since more women have undertaken paid work and concluding that we should discourage women from working to reduce the juvenile crime rate. This is not to say that there can never be **causal links** between factors that correlate. Divorce has increased over the same period that fewer people have attended places of worship and it **may** be that divorcees are less concerned about the ethics of dissolving their marriages than people in the past who made what they felt were binding vows before God. But we cannot be sure of this link simply because there is a correlation. We would need to seek further evidence to establish cause and effect. This flaw in reasoning is sometimes known as **correlation equals cause confusion**.

Alternatively the more general term **false cause** could be used. This describes any situation in which a factor or event is claimed to have caused another, without appropriate evidence being supplied, whether or not correlations are involved.

A similar error is to assume the **direction** of cause and effect. If a high proportion of clinically depressed people are found to be unemployed, employers might be accused of discriminating against those with mental illnesses. However, it might be that the people's depression resulted from their unemployment and not the other way round. This is best described as **confusing cause and effect**.

Another error is the **oversimplifying of causal relationships**. It was suggested above that the UK increase in divorce could potentially be linked with lower rates of attendance at places of worship. However, to claim a simple case of cause and effect would be quite wrong. For one thing, attendance at places of worship is not a clear indicator of attitudes. People may attend because they are expected to or may not attend despite having faith. Secondly there are multiple causes for the increase in divorce, including changes in legislation that have made it easier, legal aid and greater opportunities for women to work and therefore cope independently. To ascribe any effect to one simple cause is often poor reasoning.

1.8 *Tu quoque*

This Latin term means 'you too'. The flaw involves deflecting what might be sound criticism by accusing the critic of being guilty of the same or a similar fault. For example, if the police stopped you for driving over the speed limit, you might try arguing that the police also exceed the limit. A variation is the argument that others do it, such as ambulance drivers, or that 'everyone's doing it'. Sometimes you may see this flaw referred to as 'reasoning from wrong actions' or 'two wrongs don't make a right'. The latter is a useful phrase that explains why it is not a sound type of reasoning. Another point of criticism is that some people may be exempt from the usual rules (such as police and ambulance drivers when it comes to speeding) whereas the person accused has no such excuse.

1.9 Confusing necessary and sufficient conditions

A necessary condition is one that is vital in order for something to happen, e.g. a university might say in its prospectus that an A-level in physics is necessary to be considered for an engineering degree course. A sufficient condition is one that guarantees that the next step can follow. For example, that same university might make you an offer that, providing you get an A in physics and mathematics and at least a B in chemistry and critical thinking, they will accept you. You should be able to see the difference between the minimum without which you have no hope of being considered (necessary) and the considerably greater achievement that is enough (sufficient) to guarantee you a place. The common mistake here is for optimists to think that, because they have the minimum necessary qualification, this will be sufficient to admit them.

Some restaurants have a sign up to say that, to be admitted, men must wear ties. It is unlikely though that they would be welcomed wearing only ties!

1.10 Hasty or unwarranted or sweeping generalisation

This is a broad claim based on a limited amount of evidence or experience. A recent *Daily Mail* headline (25 April 2008) is an example:

Cheap drugs, satellite TV, free telephone calls and breakfast in bed, no wonder…

CRIMINALS BREAK <u>IN</u> TO OUR SOFT JAILS

This story was based on one drug dealer climbing over the wall of Eversthorpe Prison in Yorkshire in order to pass drugs to inmates. By using the word 'jails' in the plural,

the newspaper is suggesting the situation is far more widespread that it really is. (It is also implying false cause, giving the impression that criminals break in to prison because it is luxurious enough for them to want to stay there, whereas in fact the dealer in question only climbed in to do business.)

In the examination the context in which you may be most likely to encounter generalisations could be when an argument is based on evidence from a small survey sample or a limited number of institutions.

1.11 Straw person (also known as 'straw man')

This refers to exaggerating a possible drawback of a proposed scheme or some less attractive attribute of some of its supporters and using this as a reason for dismissing the whole scheme without further examination. The name is metaphorical. It relates to the notion of building up a large, very fragile model of just one negative aspect of the argument (like a man of straw) and then blowing it down. This is poor reasoning because very good schemes may have one or two weaknesses, for instance there may be minority groups for whom exemptions have to be made, but the ideas should be considered on the strength of their merits as well as their limitations. Here is an example:

> Imagine how many people would die in accidents and fires and of critical medical conditions if the emergency services were only allowed to respond to their calls for help by driving at less than 20 miles per hour. We would be little better than murderers if we imposed these restrictions on those rushing to help others. We should strongly oppose any attempt to impose speed limits on motorists.

In this example, the arguer has not considered any of the advantages of speed restrictions on roads, only a disadvantage that applies in a special case. This is not a sound reason for abandoning speed restrictions, as it is possible to make an exception in the case of emergency vehicles.

1.12 *Ad hominem*

Meaning 'to the man' in Latin, this refers to criticising some irrelevant feature of the arguer so that listeners dismiss his or her argument without giving it serious consideration. Such comments are frequently made in the House of Commons. When an MP makes a suggestion for new legislation, opponents sometimes remind listeners of one of his or her previous misjudgements rather than considering the new idea on its merits. While this might be a reasonable response if the proposed legislation is very similar to a failed scheme handled by that MP in the past, it is not valid for a completely different proposal. It might be that the attack is about a sexual scandal, whereas the MP's suggestion is about road building.

Students sometimes confuse *ad hominem* and straw person because both ignore the merits of an argument, resorting to ridicule instead. Generally they can be distinguished because *ad hominem* suggests something unworthy about the proposer of the idea whereas straw man exaggerates one of its limitations. However, sometimes there is a genuine overlap when fun is poked at the more eccentric members of an organisation, implying thereby that its beliefs must be as odd as its members.

> The people protesting against the Scientology Movement in Charing Cross Road were all wearing identical green masks. It's really not worth investigating the ideas of people who get up to such antics.

2 *Appeals*

An appeal is simply a reference made in an attempt to support an argument. For example, you might appeal to your listeners' humanity to support your fund-raising efforts to help Chinese earthquake victims or appeal to their knowledge of physics to follow a scientific argument.

In critical thinking we are particularly interested in fallacious appeals, rhetorical devices that are sometimes divided between misdirected appeals and emotional appeals, though there can be a degree of overlap.

2.1 Misdirected or irrelevant appeals

These may mislead us by using evidence inappropriately to support an argument. They include the following:

Appeal to authority

This is an attempt to support a conclusion on the basis that a well-known figure believes it. The claim may be weakened if the celebrity is not an expert in that particular field or if there could be other experts holding an opposing view. Sometimes the authority said to support the claim is not named, so it is impossible to check the credentials of the 'expert'.

Appeal to tradition

This device is usually used to oppose a suggested change. The arguer suggests that something which has served us well in the past should not be phased out. However, it may be that the old way of doing things is not appropriate to current circumstances. This appeal is often tinged with emotion; nostalgia for the past. However, also beware of its opposite; the appeal to novelty much loved by advertisers. New products are not automatically better than old ones.

Appeal to history

Though this phrase is sometimes used instead of 'appeal to tradition', it has a second usage. This is where evidence about what happened in the past is used to predict future performance or behaviour. This may influence decisions that are made, for example, on how to avert an impending crisis. While it might seem sensible to 'learn from our past mistakes', exactly the same situation rarely if ever recurs. Tactics used to counter an international threat in one century might not necessarily be effective in the next. Britain reduced the problem of prison overcrowding in previous centuries by trans-porting convicts to Australia but it is not a practical solution in the twenty-first century.

Appeal to popularity

Sometimes known as the appeal to common practice, this uses weight of numbers as evidence that a claim must be true or a type of behaviour acceptable. History is full of examples of wide-scale human error, such as the belief that the earth was flat, and of massive moral aberration, such as the Nazi holocaust and the slave trade. Clearly the fact that many people believe or endorse something does not guarantee that it is true or right, although consensus is sometimes significant enough to be taken into account when reaching a judgement.

2.2 Emotional appeals

Well-reasoned arguments, such as those in some pressure group or charity leaflets, might arouse a certain amount of feeling as well as providing compelling evidence why we should support their cause. However, claims that substitute **appeals to emotion** for rational argument are regarded as flawed. To escape criticism arguments must always be supported by sound reasoning and evidence.

Political leaflets and broadcasts sometimes appeal to our sense of **fear**, using scare tactics about the folly of the current party in power to persuade us to support a rival. Political speakers sometimes use an incident such as a high-profile murder as a 'political football' to kick around in public, creating a moral panic out of proportion to the problem. Sometimes this is accompanied by an appeal to **prejudice** or **stereotypes** and an appeal to **hatred** or **indignation**.

An appeal to pity, unaccompanied by sound reasons why you should support the claimant's point of view, is not usually worthy of consideration. Alternatively people might try to persuade you onto their side by an appeal to loyalty (peer pressure) or by flattering you, perhaps by suggesting that they know you are perceptive enough to join them; an appeal to vanity. Language that attempts to manipulate emotion is known as **loaded** and the term **rant** refers to a persuasive passage that expresses strong emotion without coherent reasoning.

To practise what you have learnt, consider how you would assess the reasoning of the short passage below, which is about President Bush's visit to the Middle East to negotiate a democratic settlement.

> DEMOCRACY? GEORGE BUSH DOESN'T KNOW THE MEANING OF THE WORD
>
> How dare he talk about democracy when the US-backed leaders he is meeting in the Middle East include the dictator King Abdullah of Saudi Arabia, the tyrant Hosni Mubarak of Egypt, the butcher Ehud Olmert of Israel and the stooge Nouri al Maliki in Iraq?
>
> (Extract from the *Socialist Worker*, 19 January 2008, Issue 2084, **www.socialistworker.co.uk**)

Clearly this passage contains appeals to emotion. The rhetorical question 'How dare he?' is intended to arouse indignation in the reader and the words 'dictator', 'butcher' and 'stooge' evoke fear and dislike. This prevents the reader from seriously considering whether the meeting could nevertheless be successful. No objective evidence is provided that these leaders are as corrupt as the writer asserts and a coherent conclusion is not reached, so the passage is virtually a rant.

Can the dismissal of Bush's claim be described as an example of *ad hominem*? There are certainly a number of personal attacks in the passage. However, the leaders' reputations for being undemocratic relate closely to the implied conclusion, that a democratic agreement will not be achieved, whereas the *ad hominem* flaw occurs when the accusation is irrelevant to the topic being discussed. A negative comment about Bush's own personality, such as his reputation for vocabulary confusions, would be a clearer example of *ad hominem*.

3 *Other types of evaluation*

3.1 Assessing the use of evidence

You should already be aware of some of the problems of interpreting statistics and evidence from research from Unit 1. Look back at this section to remind you, and then consider the passage below, listing all the reasons why the statistics for girl crime cannot be taken at face value.

> **Why girls are committing more crimes**
>
> A report today showing a sharp increase in crimes committed by girls has prompted researchers to investigate the underlying causes of this trend. Preliminary research, conducted by London's South Bank University, suggested a number of contributing factors. One reason might simply be that the overall population of girls has increased and therefore the number of crimes committed by this population could be expected to rise proportionally.
>
> According to Susannah Eagle at South Bank, the statistics released by the Youth Justice Board only took into consideration the absolute number of crimes committed by girls and not offences per person. 'It is very possible, therefore, that there might not be more girls committing offences, but that some girls are prolific offenders,' she said. The rise in reported crimes could also be due to changing social attitudes. Eagle suggested there was now a lower tolerance of minor offences.
>
> Underage drinking could also be a factor. When the research team interviewed a sample group of girls who had committed a crime, there was a statistically significant link between committing a violent offence and the recent use of alcohol.
>
> According to Enver Solomon, deputy director of the Centre for Crime and Justice Studies, 'Police are under pressure to hit certain targets. Offences committed by kids — such as fights between girls in the playground — would be more likely to be recorded now than a few years ago.'
>
> (Extract from 'Why girls are committing more crimes' by Elizabeth Stewart,
> *Guardian*, 15 May 2008, **www.guardian.co.uk**)

The above example should have reminded you of some of the reasons that statistics may be unreliable. They may be affected by changes in the overall population and they may not be sensitive enough to reveal important factors, for example failing to distinguish between more girls committing crime and more crimes by a small number of girls. They may also be affected by factors such as greater public willingness to report certain phenomena and increased activity by professionals in response to new initiatives such as target setting. (Notice that under-age drinking was the only factor mentioned in the article which could help to explain a genuine increase in the proportion of girls committing crime.)

Now see if you can answer questions assessing the evidence in the following passage.

> *Vitamins linked with prisoner behaviour*
>
> A study led by Bernard Gesch of the University of Oxford's Laboratory of Physiology, Dr Sean Hammond of the Department of Applied Psychology, University College Cork, Ireland, and fellow academics has found evidence that giving supplementary vitamins, minerals and essential fatty acids to young adult prisoners may reduce their antisocial behaviour.

Evaluating arguments

The researchers found evidence that offenders sometimes have not even heard of vitamins and consume diets lacking in essential nutrients. They hypothesised that this could adversely affect their behaviour. They then conducted trials on 231 young adult prisoners after recording the number of offences, such as violence, they had been disciplined for in prison in previous weeks.

On a random basis, some prisoners were given nutritional supplements for at least 2 weeks and others received placebos (fake supplements that looked identical). The experiment was double-blind, meaning that those recording the data were unaware of which prisoners had received genuine supplements. The result was a 26% decrease in the rate of antisocial behaviour (as measured by disciplinary incidents) in the group that received the nutritional supplements.

The experimenters suggest that the behaviour of people not in prison, such as those served with ASBOs, might also be improved if they could be persuaded to take the same nutritional supplements. The research was supported by a grant from the research charity Natural Justice. Scotia Pharmaceuticals Ltd and Unigreg Ltd supplied nutritional supplements.

(Information sourced from **bjp.rcpsych.org**)

1 Assess the degree to which the evidence provided supports the view that diets lacking in essential nutrients could adversely affect prisoner behaviour. *(3 marks)*

2 Assess the evidence for the view that the behaviour of people not in prison, such as those served with ASBOs, might also be improved if they could be persuaded to take the same nutritional supplements. *(2 marks)*

The number of marks available should suggest to you that you should try to make about three points for the first answer, or two substantial points, whereas a slightly shorter answer should be acceptable for the second question.

Your answer to the first question could include some of the following points, but of course not all of them. The evidence supporting the view that diets lacking in essential nutrients could adversely affect prisoner behaviour is strong, as prisoners who received diet supplements improved their behaviour markedly.

- The possibility of bias in assessing their behaviour was avoided by the double-blind test, meaning that those who rated their behaviour as improved were not affected by the expectation that it might be as they did not know which prisoners had received the supplements and which the placebo. In other words their assessment was unbiased.
- The sample of 231 is large enough to be fairly convincing and the participants were randomly chosen so were likely to represent a variety of prisoner personalities.
- Those conducting the experiment were experts in the appropriate field, meaning the experiment is likely to have been conducted accurately.

Possible weaknesses are as follows:

- Statistics are not provided showing whether there was any decrease in antisocial behaviour among those who received the placebo. If this also dropped, it could be that prisoners respond positively to concern being shown for their health rather than to the vitamins themselves. (Notice that this point could be used in answer to a question that asks you to suggest other conclusions that could reasonably be drawn from evidence used in an argument.)

- Being sponsored by Natural Justice, a research charity that believes nutrition affects the brain and shapes social behaviour, might have put some pressure on the research team to reach this conclusion. Likewise, there may also have been encouragement from the companies who supplied the supplements free to find evidence of their usefulness. On the other hand, the researchers were open about this sponsorship, suggesting they had nothing to hide, and it is difficult to see how their rigorous methods could have been influenced by lack of neutrality.

An answer to the second question could raise some of the following or similar points. The evidence that the behaviour of people not in prison could be improved if they could be persuaded to take nutritional supplements is less strong than the evidence above.

- No evidence is provided that people not in prison, such as those served with ASBOs have poor nutrition. While offenders were found often to 'consume diets lacking in essential nutrients', and this may well be the case with those people served with ASBOs who are from deprived backgrounds, we cannot be certain of this. Some people served with ASBOs come from prosperous backgrounds where nutrition may be good.
- The claim that the behaviour of people not in prison, such as those served with ASBOs, might also be improved by supplements is not backed by research, only by an extrapolation from the prisoner experiment.
- An analogy is being implied between the likely effects on prisoners and the likely effect on those with ASBOs, but relevant similarities between these groups are not established.
- The claim is a hypothetical statement so it is only guesswork.

On the other hand, the word 'might' means that a limited claim is being made, and it is justified to suggest that this is reasonably likely to be true. The conclusion is therefore not overdrawn.

3.2 Assessing analogies

As explained above, using analogies in arguments involves the creation of parallels, reasoning that what is true for one situation must be true of another which is, supposedly, similar. Evaluating an analogy requires you to gauge whether the situations being compared really are similar enough for the conclusion to be reached. Read the following passage, which contains an analogy, and try to form an initial judgement.

> Britain has very strict laws about testing the health of domestic pets before letting them into the country. Even British people living in France, whenever they want to take their dog to Britain for a few days, have to take it to the vet's in order to have its health checked and a certificate issued. The code on the certificate has to correspond with a microchip in the dog to avoid the possibility of fraud. With the increased incidence in Britain of diseases such as tuberculosis, prevalent abroad but virtually eradicated here until recently, there is an obvious need for compulsory health checks and certification for people entering the country, even if they are British and have been away for a few days on holiday.

Questions about analogies often come in pairs. In this situation, the questions would probably be something like this:

- Identify what is being compared in the analogy in paragraph X. *(2 marks)*
- How well does the analogy support the author's argument? *(3 marks)*

You could answer the first question by saying the precautions taken to prevent animals from abroad bringing diseases to Britain are being likened to the need for similar precautions for people entering Britain. This answer is precise and detailed enough to be worthy of 2 marks. A briefer and vaguer answer, that animals are being compared to people, would be less well rewarded. The short answer is far too general, as animals are not being likened to people in any other way than the one just stated, as potential bearers of disease.

Assessing the effectiveness of an analogy is a longer process, requiring several points to be made:

- You will be expected to discuss important ways in which the situations are similar and dissimilar, identifying at least one point for each.
- Often you may feel that the situations being compared are less similar than the writer implies, so that you would state that the differences are significant enough to weaken the analogy and therefore the argument is flawed.
- Occasionally you may think that a statement about the supposedly uncontroversial situation is inaccurate or too sweeping.
- After discussion, conclude by stating whether the writer provided a persuasive and effective analogy, or a disanalogy (a poor analogy) that fails to support the argument.

In the example provided you might argue that:

- Domestic pets and people are similar in that both can have communicable diseases that present a health risk to others.
- However, there are significant differences in the situation.
- A relatively small number of pets travel to and fro, and because this is a fairly unusual situation their owners are prepared to put up with the expense and trouble incurred. In contrast a high proportion of the British public go abroad on holidays and for work and there would be major protests if health checks were introduced. The inconvenience would be felt to outweigh the risks.
- We have different attitudes to animal rights and to human rights and dignity. Animals are unable to object to having microchips inserted whereas many humans would.
- These differences outweigh the similarities between the two situations, making the analogy a weak one that therefore fails to support the argument.
- If you were to reach the opposite conclusion as a result of finding more parallels between the situations, your answer, if convincing, would be equally rewarded.

3.3 Evaluating examples

Evaluating examples requires similar skills to evaluating analogies. Consider whether the example is:

- typical enough to support the argument well
- an unusual one, with the result that readers would feel the need for further examples before accepting the conclusion
- so ill-chosen that it acts as a counter-example, undermining the conclusion.

Try to assess this example:

> British and US politicians aren't evil people, they just think their country would be a terrible mess without them. They begin to think they're so valuable they become prepared to do bad things to stay in power. You can see that with Robert Mugabe. If he'd quit 15 years ago, he'd still be the hero of liberation of Zimbabwe. Instead he's a monster.

(Gavin Esler in *Metro*, 15 May 2008)

You might comment that this is really an analogy rather than an example, as Mugabe is not a British or US politician but an African leader. The example is poor in other ways, because Mugabe's behaviour is so extreme that it cannot reasonably be likened to any actions British and US politicians are known to have made to retain their positions. The reader is likely to require further examples closer to home to convince us that our politicians 'become prepared to do bad things to stay in power'. This example therefore, because it is so untypical, serves little purpose, except as an emotional appeal.

3.4 Evaluating explanations and suggesting alternatives

In the Unit 2 exam, you might be asked to assess explanations, either in the form of multiple-choice options or within a longer passage, or to offer reasonable alternatives. Consider the four explanations for the trends in divorce given below.

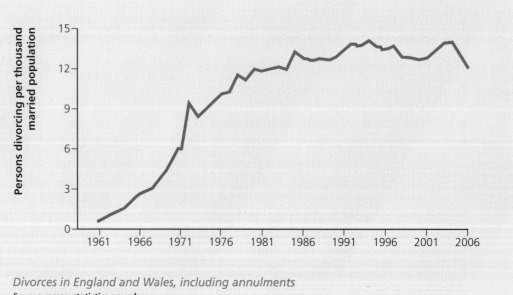

Divorces in England and Wales, including annulments
Source: **www.statistics.gov.uk**

1 Which of the following statements is the *least* convincing explanation of the trends shown in the graph, which shows the number of divorces granted each year in thousands?
   (a) The number of divorces may have increased during the 1960s in response to growing feminist awareness, which could have encouraged married women to question their situations.
   (b) The Divorce Reform Act passed in 1969 in England and Wales came into effect in 1971. As this made divorce easier, it explains the steep peak in divorces in 1971.

(c) The brief downturn in the number of divorces around 1973 could be explained because most of those who had been waiting for divorces for some years had acted quickly when the Divorce Reform Act was implemented.

(d) The steady decline in church-going during the twentieth century is reflected in increased divorce, as people are less concerned than they used to be about keeping vows made before God.

2 Suggest an explanation of your own for the downward trend in divorce since about 1993.

The correct answer to question 1 is (d). Although there has been a steady decline in church attendance, the graph does not indicate a steady increase in divorce but a much more varied pattern. The other answers offer better explanations for specific patterns in the graph. In addition, decline in church-going does not necessarily indicate a loss of religious beliefs and in Britain a proportion of the population attends other places of worship.

For question 2, a sensible suggestion to explain the general downward trend in divorce since about 1993 could be the fact that fewer couples are getting married, as living together has become more socially acceptable.

3.5 Assessing hypothetical reasoning

Unit 1 introduced you to hypothetical reasoning. Glance back at pages 8–9 to remind yourself of the problems of using this type of reasoning to support an argument. Predictions about the future are based on guesswork so can only provide limited support. An example is as follows:

> If the rate of obesity increases at its present rate, then we shall soon need to redesign furniture and seating in public transport and places of entertainment to accommodate bigger people.

In fact this may not be necessary, as obesity rates may fall as people learn more about its risks and how to avoid it.

Hypothesising about how the present might have turned out if the past had been different is even more fruitless, as this is speculation about something which can have no basis in reality.

A different type of hypothetical reasoning that is sometimes known as **suppositional reasoning** may be more worthwhile. It is used by scientists, doctors and detectives and other types of investigators.

> Suppose that the murderer had entered and left the scene of the crime via the window. If that were the case then the window would not be locked from the inside, unless the murderer had an accomplice, which has been ruled out. However, investigation has revealed that the window was locked from the inside. The murderer must then have taken a different route or still be in the building.

This type of hypothesis is based on deduction about alternative real-life possibilities. Similarly a doctor might work out that if her patient had a certain disease he would be likely to exhibit particular symptoms. As he has no such symptoms, then it is necessary to search for other symptoms that match a different diagnosis.

When assessing the extent to which hypothetical reasoning supports an argument, you will need to judge whether it is based on ill-informed guesswork or a more logical process of considering the evidence for a series of different possibilities.

3.6 Assessing the relevance of general principles

General principles were initially explained in Unit 1 (see page 9) and expanded upon earlier in this section (see pages 29–30). Refer back to these if necessary. You may be asked to assess the extent to which a particular principle applies to other situations or to explain where a general principle would not be applicable.

For example, if there were a passage about people protesting in public, you should be able to identify that the right to do this in Britain reflects the principle of free speech. What other situations can you think of where such a principle applies?

Good examples would be UK radio and television interviews, where people likely to express contrasting views are invited to put them forward. The freedom of the press and the rights of victims to express their feelings at the end of a court case are further examples. However, the general principle is not applicable if people wish to stir up racial hatred and there are a number of laws restricting what can be said on matters of defence. In this type of question you might be required to do some creative thinking, seeking examples from your own general knowledge, or relevant situations might be mentioned in the passage.

4   *Tips for answering evaluation questions*

- There may be up to 3 marks available for assessing the argument in a particular paragraph and it is important to try to earn all the marks. A rough guide is to make one point per mark. The amount of space allocated will also give you an idea of the amount of detail required.
- The best answers usually include specialist vocabulary, so ensure that you name the flaw or strength (unless that information is provided in the question).
- Usually it is also necessary to define the flaw and to explain how it is arising in this particular case.
- Sometimes, as in the case of unjustified assumptions and other types of erroneous judgement, it is useful to indicate what the truth might be.
- It is important to strike a balance between completing the paper in time and answering so briefly that you score only half marks for questions to which you know the answer.
- You are strongly advised to try answering a variety of questions from the Unit 2 specimen paper in writing and then comparing your work with the examples on the mark scheme. You should be able to access both the specimen paper and the mark scheme on the OCR website. You may be quite shocked to see the amount of detail required for full marks. Alternatively it may reassure you that your answers are thorough enough. Either way it is essential to know, as good timing is one of the most critical factors in examinations.

5 Tips for multiple-choice questions

The Unit 2 paper consists of a number of short passages and a few graphs, charts or diagrams, followed by multiple-choice questions with four options. Some of the passages may generate more than one set of questions. You will answer them by marking the appropriate letter on a sheet that can be scanned by an optical mark reader. The questions will test your ability to analyse the structure of arguments (AO1) and to assess arguments and evidence (AO2). Until real examination papers for this specification become available, you will find past papers from the previous Unit 2 specification on the OCR website helpful for multiple-choice questions, although there are none containing visual material.

To be confident about answering the questions, brush up on your skills in the following areas:
- Distinguishing an argument from other material such as explanations, rants or collections of facts. An argument is a coherent attempt to persuade, with a conclusion supported by at least one relevant reason.
- Deciding which is the best statement of the main conclusion of the passage. This often means distinguishing it from the intermediate conclusion and from summaries which are imprecise.
- Deciding which of a number of options best supports or most weakens the argument in the passage.
- Deciding which statement is an underlying assumption or principle.
- Identifying the best statement of the flaw in a passage. The options here may be technical terms such as *ad hominem* and straw person.
- Identifying the best statement of the intermediate conclusion or counter-assertion in the passage. This involves analysing the passage to identify the named component and then choosing the option exactly the same in meaning.
- Deciding which of a number of options is closest to the meaning of a particular word used in the passage. This tests your awareness of the ambiguity of terms.
- Scrutinising a graph or chart and answering questions about which a number of options could be an explanation for the results or could reliably be inferred from the data.
- Reading a brief argument and choosing which one of four lists or diagrams of components (making use of common notations such as R1, C, Ev and CA) accurately conveys its structure.

It is a good idea to look at the question first before reading the passage. This focuses your mind straight away on what you are looking for. Then read the passage and decide what you think the answer is before reading the options. You are then less likely to be distracted by options that are wrong.

The process of elimination approach is only recommended if you have little idea about what the answer could be. There is often one answer that is the opposite of the correct one, one that is not very relevant and two which are very similar, one of which is the 'best statement' of the answer. Identify the exact difference in meaning between the options to select the correct one. If you really cannot decide, choose one of the better options randomly and move on, as you need to spend not much more than 1 minute per question in order to leave adequate time for Sections B and C.

C Developing your own arguments

Section C of the Unit 2 paper requires some fairly basic creative thinking on your part, going beyond information that is provided in the passage, as well as good skills in written communication (AO3). To start with you may be required to perform one or two very short writing tasks, making suggestions that in some way relate to the passage you have just read or a parallel situation, but which require a little imagination.

For example, you may be asked for a possible explanation for a phenomenon which the author has mentioned in passing, or to supply an additional reason beyond those given in the passage. This might involve providing some evidence to back up your reason. You could be asked to suggest a principle that could underlie the argument in a particular paragraph, an additional example to illustrate a particular point or a counter-example. Drawing on your experience of analogies, you could be asked to assess how similar a particular situation would be to one described in the passage.

1 *Writing your own arguments*

Your main tasks will be to write your own arguments, probably two.

These arguments are likely to carry more marks than questions in Sections A and B, so keep a close eye on the time throughout the examination. If you are falling behind, write the arguments well before the end and then go back to the remaining lower-mark questions.

At least one question is likely to ask you to construct a further argument either challenging or supporting the main conclusion of the passage. As you will not be told what the conclusion is, it is important not to mix it up with the intermediate conclusion, although a good argument based on the wrong conclusion should still gain some marks.

Once you have identified the conclusion, make sure that you use this exact wording in your argument. Students often drift to a conclusion that is similar but not exactly the same as the one provided, for example from discouraging cars to banning them, and this type of inaccuracy can cost you marks. Others forget to include the conclusion as they have mentioned it in their title, losing marks as a result.

Writing a **further** argument means that you must not repeat the reasons, evidence or examples used in the original passage. The only situation in which this might be acceptable would be if you were to take an ambiguous piece of evidence and cleverly interpret it in the opposite way from the original passage.

If given a choice, you may find it easier to challenge the argument in the passage than to support it, as many of the most obvious reasons supporting it will already have been given.

Make your decision totally clear to the examiner by heading your work 'An argument challenging…' or 'An argument supporting…', rather than adopting a more imaginative title.

You will be told which components or elements your argument should include. These are likely to be:

- a main conclusion
- three or more reasons that support an intermediate or main conclusion
- an intermediate conclusion
- use of evidence or examples to support the argument
- counter-assertion or counter-argument

and possibly elements such as:
- hypothetical reasoning
- a general principle
- an analogy

Ensure that you include all the components listed in the instructions. If you have time, it is advisable to supply more than the bare minimum. Your work will be allocated to a mark band and the highest level requires the candidate to supply a developed argument that contains 'at least' three reasons, 'at least' one intermediate conclusion and so on. A fuller argument is therefore welcomed, providing it is carefully constructed and convincing. However, do not spend so long on the first argument that you are unable to complete the second.

The lines on the paper indicate roughly how long your arguments are expected to be. On the specimen paper about three-quarters of an A4 page of wide lines were allocated for each argument.

Plan a clear structure for your argument before you start writing. A long, confused ramble will not be well rewarded. You could make jottings in pencil on the blank page at the back of the examination paper to work out your argument. Rub or cross out these notes before giving in your paper.

For the second argument you may be supplied with a conclusion in some way related to the topic of the passage but not its main focus. For example, a principle might be identified that is mentioned in the passage and you could be asked to consider a variety of situations in which the principle might be applied and then construct an argument that either supports or challenges this principle.

You are not expected to have extensive prior knowledge of the topic used in stimulus material. In choosing evidence or examples, you should draw on your own general knowledge.

The convincing nature of your arguments will be judged as well as the structure, so avoid including flippant reasons and evidence that is clearly made up. A top-band argument must rely only on one or two reasonable assumptions. The reasons, evidence and examples must fully support the intermediate conclusions and overall conclusion.

Check your work for accuracy of grammar, spelling and punctuation as these are assessed in this part of the paper.

Unless a different structure is specified, examiners are likely to be impressed by a sound argument with the following or similar components, clearly structured as follows:
- CA (counter-argument)
- RCA (response to counter-argument)
- R1

- Ev
- R2
- Ex
- IC1
- R3
- Ev
- R4
- Ex
- IC2
- R5
- Ev
- C

2   *Planning your arguments*

A useful tip in planning your argument is to work backwards from the conclusion you wish to support. Suppose this is:

> Education should be made compulsory to the age of 18.

As two intermediate conclusions will show your ability to create a sophisticated argument, *assuming there is time for this in the examination*, think of two major, broad reasons that could support the conclusion. These could be:

> Education for self-development

and:

> Benefits to the economy

If these are going to be your **intermediate conclusions**, you need to think of reasons that could lead on to these. Try breaking down the notion of the education for self-development into two or more elements. These could be gaining independent study skills and preparation for everyday life. These ideas could be phrased as **reasons**, but they will need **examples** or **evidence** to support them.

Once you have worked that out, consider how you could work back from the other intermediate conclusion about benefits to the economy. Think of two relevant factors that can be developed into reasons, with some examples or evidence you have perhaps heard in the media.

Can you think of any further reasons why education should be extended to 18? It could relieve the problem of unemployment among 16 and 17 year olds. This reason could be included towards the end of your argument.

Before we put it all together, a **counter-argument** is needed, followed by a **response** to it to push the argument back in the direction we want to go. How about referring to the fact that many young people dislike school?

The resulting argument could emerge as follows. Each component has been set out on a new line to help you analyse it. Check it over to see if you can recognise all the components.

Developing your own arguments

An argument supporting the view that education should be made compulsory to the age of 18

There has been some opposition to the raising of the school leaving age to 18 because many young people dislike school.

However, there has been opposition to every attempt to extend education since 1870, however beneficial.

Most students develop the independent study skills needed for later life after their mid-teens.

Research suggests that in the early secondary years they regard their teachers as the main source of knowledge and it is not until later that they begin to think for themselves.

Furthermore young people need to learn not only facts but about abstract matters relating to adult life such as current affairs, ethics and other life and leisure skills. Psychologists suggest abstract reasoning is best accomplished in the later teens.

So continuing education to 18 is essential for young people's self-development as independent learners fully prepared for the adult world.

An extra 2 years at school could provide students with additional vocational skills needed in the modern workplace, particularly computing and less familiar languages such as Mandarin and Arabic.

Social skills, such as learning to solve problems effectively in teams, would teach them to work effectively with others.

Therefore extending education would benefit the economy by better preparing young people for work.

This proposal would also relieve the current problem of unemployed 16 and 17 year olds who are doing nothing to advance their own potential.

Thus there are a number of compelling reasons why education should be made compulsory to the age of 18.

In case you had problems analysing the argument, this is the solution:

An argument supporting the view that education should be made compulsory to the age of 18

There has been some opposition to the raising of the school leaving age to eighteen because many young people dislike school (CA). However, there has been opposition to every attempt to extend education since 1870, however beneficial (RCA).

Most students usually develop the independent study skills needed for later life after their mid-teens (R1). Research suggests that in the early secondary years they regard their teachers as the main source of knowledge and it is not until later that they begin to think for themselves (Ev). Furthermore young people need to learn not only facts but about abstract matters relating to adult life (R2) such as current affairs, ethics and other life and leisure skills (Ex). Psychologists suggest abstract reasoning is best accomplished in the later teens (Ev). So continuing education to 18 is essential for young people's self-development as independent learners fully prepared for the adult world (IC1).

An extra 2 years at school could provide students with additional vocational skills needed in the modern workplace (R3), particularly computing and less familiar languages such as Mandarin and Arabic (Ex). Social skills, such as learning to solve problems effectively in teams, would teach them to work effectively with others (R4 and Ex). Therefore extending education would benefit the economy by better preparing young people for work (IC2).

This proposal would also relieve the current problem of unemployed 16 and 17 year olds who are doing nothing to advance their own potential (R5).

Thus there are a number of compelling reasons why education should be made compulsory to the age of 18 (C).

Unless you are a quick worker, it is unlikely that you would be able to manage two arguments of such length in the time allowed, and of course it is better to complete two shorter ones that still fulfil the minimum requirements than to be unable to complete the paper. You could save time by supplying evidence and examples for fewer reasons or by providing only one reason instead of two to support one of the intermediate conclusions. A compromise if you do not have many minutes left could be to construct your first argument based on the minimum requirements and to make the second argument fuller if time permits.

Clearly it is essential to practise writing arguments to a strict time-limit. Unless OCR changes the examination details after publishing the specification (check this for yourself to make sure), the recommended time for completing Sections B and C of the Unit 2 paper is 1 hour and 10 minutes. Sections B and C carry similar marks, so it is worth putting a considerable amount of effort into your arguments in Section C. Try a Section B question and see if you can complete it in 30–35 minutes. Assuming it takes you 5 minutes to complete one or two low-mark questions in Section C, this should then leave you about half an hour to divide between the two arguments.

Try writing an argument now in timed conditions, using a similar structure to the one above. As well as having a title stating explicitly which option you have chosen, your argument must include:

- a clearly stated main conclusion
- three or more reasons that support an intermediate or main conclusion
- at least one intermediate conclusion
- use of evidence or examples to support the argument
- counter-assertion or counter-argument

Identify each element of your argument with the usual notations and get a teacher or an able fellow student to check it and give you feedback. Your argument could support or challenge one of the following conclusions, the last of which is a general principle:

- The age for buying and consuming alcohol should be raised to 21.
- The government was right to increase the age for purchasing cigarettes to 18.
- The voting age should be reduced to 16.
- There should be much stiffer penalties for carrying knives.
- Understanding offenders' motivation is more crucial than increasing penalties.

Keep working at this to see how elaborate a structure you can manage in the time allocation of about 15 minutes. Check your work against these OCR criteria for a top-level argument:

Criteria for top-level marks

- Candidates present their own relevant further argument with a clear structure that includes at least three reasons and at least one properly supported intermediate conclusion.
- The argument is persuasive and relies only on one or two reasonable assumptions.
- The argument will also contain evidence/examples that support the argument.
- There may be a counter-argument/counter-examples.
- The final conclusion is precisely stated.
- Grammar, spelling and punctuation are good. Errors are few.

D Revision checklist for Unit 2

Remember to revise what you have studied for Unit F501: Introduction to Critical thinking as some of the information and skills will be needed again in Unit 2.

1 *The examination*

OCR codes
- AS Critical Thinking subject code: H052
- Unit 2 code: F502

Mark allocation
75 marks, 50% of the total AS GCE marks. Section A is worth a maximum of 15 marks, Sections B and C are worth 30 marks each.

Timing
1 hour 30 minutes. You are advised to spend no more than 20 minutes on the multiple-choice questions. If you then spend no more than 30 minutes on Section B, you could spend a few minutes on the shorter questions in Section C and half an hour on writing your arguments. Ideally leave a little time for checking your work.

Practicalities
For the Section A multiple-choice questions remember to take a pencil to fill in the OMR sheet.

Write your answers for Sections B and C in black ink in the spaces provided on the question paper.

This paper has three sections and candidates should answer all the questions:
- Section A: Multiple choice. Questions are based on passages, charts or diagrams. The material may provide the stimulus for one or more questions.
- Section B: Analysing and evaluating argument. Analyse the structure and evaluate the reasoning of a passage of approximately 500 words containing an argument, responding with short answers.
- Section C: Developing your own arguments. In addition to answering a couple of short questions, write one or more further arguments of your own in response to the passage provided.

2 *Section A: Multiple choice*

Some of the questions in Section A require analysis (AO1) of the structure of a short passage asking, for example, which of the four options given below is the conclusion of the passage.

A variation, which requires more than simple recognition, is the type of question asking which of several quite similar options is the best statement of the conclusion that could be drawn from the passage.

Some of the analysis questions may feature components not taught in Unit 1, such as intermediate conclusions, and less obvious ones such as hypothetical reasoning and analogies.

Other questions require evaluation skills (AO2). They may ask you to identify the flaw in the passage, either from a list of explanations or from a list of technical names for flaws.

A variation is the type of question asking which of a series of pieces of evidence, if true, would most strengthen or weaken the argument in the passage. A few questions may test your understanding of the content of diagrams, charts or graphs.

3 Section B: Analysing and evaluating argument

For Section B you will be required to read a document and answer a few questions identifying components of the argument (AO1) and rather more questions evaluating it (AO2), considering weaknesses and strengths in the reasoning.

3.1 Analysis

You will need to recall the elements of argument covered in Unit 1, such as **conclusion, reason, evidence, example, counter-argument** and **assumption**.

In addition you should be able to identify and explain the purpose of the following components within an argument in the source material:
- intermediate conclusion
- analogy
- general principle

The specification requires you to be able to explain the difference between an explanation and an argument and to recognise that longer passages may contain explanations as part of the reasoning.

You should also be able to demonstrate understanding of a range of specific terms and use them accurately according to their usage in critical thinking. (Bear in mind the difference between the way the term 'assumption' is used in this subject, as opposed to its everyday use.) The terms listed by OCR for this unit are:
- counter
- challenge
- assess
- opinion
- belief
- knowledge
- reasoning
- refute
- repudiate
- infer and inference
- contradict and contradiction
- coherent
- structure
- strength and weakness
- support
- inconsistent and inconsistency
- consistent

- imply
- converse
- ambiguous
- drawing a conclusion

3.2 Evaluation

You will be expected to evaluate parts of the argument in the document, identifying strengths and weaknesses in its reasoning. In doing so, you should demonstrate an understanding of the difference between challenging reasoning with counter-arguments or alternative explanations, and the more complex skill of explaining the strengths and weaknesses of the original reasoning.

You may need to evaluate arguments by drawing on types of evaluation introduced in Unit 1 such as assessing the use of evidence.

Flaws

Flaws are common but erroneous patterns of reasoning where the conclusion is very unlikely to follow from the reasons given. You should be able to identify flaws by name and clarify how you have recognised them in this particular context. You must also be capable of explaining why a given conclusion is unlikely to follow from the reasons given because of a flaw in the argument, in other words why such reasoning is flawed.

You should be able to recognise the following flaws within an argument in source material:
- slippery slope
- post hoc
- circular argument (begging the question)
- false dichotomy or restricting the options or choices
- conflation
- false cause/confusing cause and effect/simplifying causal relationships
- reasoning from wrong actions (*tu quoque* or 'two wrongs don't make a right')
- confusing necessary and sufficient conditions
- hasty or unwarranted or sweeping generalisation
- straw person (also known as 'straw man')
- *ad hominem*
- arguing from one thing to another, unrelated conclusion

Appeals

You should be able to identify an 'appeal', a rhetorical device swaying the audience by emotional persuasion rather than by rational argument. This means it may not support the conclusion of an argument as effectively as logical reasoning. Ensure that you can identify by name and describe the following appeals within arguments:
- appeal to authority
- appeal to tradition
- appeal to history
- appeal to popularity
- appeal to emotion, specifying the type of emotion that is aroused

Other types of evaluation

You should be able to assess strengths and weaknesses within arguments by:

- assessing the use of evidence in the form of survey and other research data, statistics (percentages or proportions), statistical representations (average or mean) and other numerical information (This is also required for Unit 1)
- evaluating the use of analogies within arguments by:
  - identifying the situations compared in the analogy and the conclusion drawn from the parallel reasoning
  - identifying similarities and dissimilarities between the situations and assessing their significance
  - reaching a judgement about whether the analogy is strong enough to support the conclusion drawn in the argument
- identifying and assessing examples used in the argument, by commenting on the relevance of the example (which may be good or poor, even a counter-example), and by assessing the degree to which the example helps the author to make the point
- identifying explanations given within an argument and offering reasonable alternatives
- suggesting other conclusions that could reasonably be drawn from evidence used in an argument
- assessing the extent to which any hypothetical reasoning supports an argument
- assessing the extent to which general principles apply in other situations and explaining where a general principle would not be applicable

4 Section C: Developing your own arguments

In Section C there may be a couple of lower-mark questions inviting your own ideas about some aspect of the passage, for example asking you to suggest explanations for some phenomenon mentioned in it or further examples or reasons.

However, your main task will be to write your own arguments (AO3), probably two, that relate to the conclusion of the argument in the document or an allied theme. You may have to challenge or support the conclusion of the stimulus passage or a conclusion stated in the question. Clear structure is important as well as ensuring that the content of an argument clearly supports the conclusion given with only a few reasonable assumptions being needed.

To score high marks your argument needs to include a range of argument components, for example:
- three or more reasons that support an intermediate or main conclusion
- an intermediate conclusion
- use of evidence or examples to support the argument
- counter-assertion or counter-argument
- possibly elements such as hypothetical reasoning, general principle or analogy

It is important to:
- support the precise conclusion required, not a variation
- state in your title what the purpose of your argument is (supporting or challenging what conclusion)
- use convincing reasons and evidence drawn from your own general knowledge, not ones from the passage

UNIT 3 Ethical reasoning and decision making

The documents that accompany the Unit 3 examination present a variety of facts and views about a controversial issue relating to medical ethics, crime and punishment, the environment or some other area of social or political concern. The examination is likely to begin with some questions requiring short answers and then lead you gradually towards two longer essay tasks, applying a range of criteria to potential decisions and eventually reaching a judgement about which course of action to take. As the bulk of the marks are awarded for these two essays, it is important not to spend more than a few minutes on the short questions.

A Answering the short questions

1 Analysing problems of definition

It is likely that one of the first questions on the Unit 3 paper will ask you to identify problems of defining a particular term that is crucial to the issue being discussed. Different documents may include explicit but contradictory definitions or the key term may be used without definition, leaving you to interpret the intended shade of meaning, which again is likely to vary between documents.

As well as arriving at the differing meanings, you need to be able to identify *why* reaching a definition is problematical, asking yourself whether people holding different views on the moral issue in question would be likely to interpret the key concept in different ways. Would civil rights supporters and prison officers have the same concept of 'freedom'? Alternatively it may be that people from various educational, professional or cultural backgrounds or in a range of situations may use the term differently. You already know that those who have studied critical thinking use the word 'assumption' differently from those who have not. The 'conclusion' of a concert always means the end, whereas the 'conclusion' of an argument, while reflecting the final stage in the reasoning, can be at the beginning.

Definitions discussed may relate to quite tangible concepts such as 'speeding', which can be problematical in different circumstances. Is driving 1 mph over the limit speeding? What about driving just below the legal limit but in hazardous conditions such as fog, when the norm is to go far more slowly? In some instances, such as with 'unemployment' and 'poverty', official definitions used by particular governments change over time. Problems also arise in applying terminology across cultures. A lifestyle that is regarded as 'poor' in the UK might seem like relative wealth in sub-Saharan Africa. Usually you should be able to infer these different possibilities from the sources, though sometimes a little creative thinking is needed.

You may be presented with more abstract moral concepts such as 'duty', 'rights', 'need', 'entitlement' and 'desert'. Individuals will clearly differ in what they regard as someone's duty, depending, for example, on their religious background and upbringing or their particular circumstances.

Consider the moral concept of fairness. Exactly what do you think it means? Under recent legislation anyone over the age of 16 caught carrying a knife will face automatic prosecution, and will risk a jail sentence of up to 4 years. Supposing a person whose job it is to lay linoleum and carpets was searched by the police on his way to work and charged with possessing a knife. One media report might describe this as fair as the law must apply equally to all. However, another could object that knives are the usual tool for cutting lino and it is unfair to prosecute workers for carrying the necessities of a legal trade. In this context you would need to refer to the two documents and explain that 'fair' can mean equal treatment for all or it can refer to reasonable operation of the law, if necessary allowing for cases of special need. The problem here arises from the ambiguity of the word 'fair'.

If you are not used to thinking about the nuances (shades of meaning) of words in this manner, it is worth looking up some moral concepts in a large dictionary to make yourself aware of the range of meanings found in different contexts. For example, in the *Reader's Digest Universal Dictionary*, definitions for 'fair' include words relevant to the situation just discussed, such as *free of favouritism or bias*, *just to all parties*, *consistent with rules*, and *honest*, as well as totally different meanings such as *clear and sunny*, *beautiful*, *of light colour* and *considerable*.

For practice, assume that you have been asked the following question:

> Using Documents 1, 2 and 3, explain why the term 'war' might present problems of definition.

Can you think of any different shades of meaning straight away?

Now look at the documents below and see if you can find at least three different usages of the word. Take note of which section in which documents provided you with these different ideas. Finally try to identify precisely why it is difficult to define the concept.

Document 1 *War*

War is a violent way for determining who gets to say what goes on in a given territory, for example, regarding: who gets power, who gets wealth and resources, whose ideals prevail, where the border rests and so on. War is the ultimate means for deciding these issues if a peaceful process or resolution can't be agreed upon.

The mere threat of war, and the presence of mutual disdain between political communities, do not suffice as indicators of war. The conflict of arms must be actual, and not merely latent, for it to count as war. Further, the actual armed conflict must be both intentional and widespread: isolated clashes between rogue officers, or border patrols, do not count as actions of war. The onset of war requires a conscious commitment, and a significant mobilization, on the part of the belligerents in question. There's no real war, so to speak, until the fighters intend to go to war and until they do so with a heavy quantum of force.

War is a brutal and ugly enterprise. Yet it remains central to human history and social change. War and its threat continue to be forces in our lives. Recent events graphically demonstrate this proposition, whether we think of the 9/11 attacks, the counter-attack on Afghanistan, the overthrow of Iraq's Saddam Hussein, the Darfur crisis in Sudan, the bombings in Madrid and London, or the on-going 'war on terror' more generally. We all had high hopes going into the new millennium in 2000; alas, this new century has already been savagely scarred with warfare.

(Extracts from the article 'War' from the Stanford Encyclopedia of Philosophy, **plato.stanford.edu/entries/war**)

Document 2   Cold War and proxy war

The **Cold War** was the period of conflict, tension and competition between the United States and the Soviet Union and their respective allies from the mid-1940s until the early 1990s. Throughout this period, the rivalry between the two superpowers unfolded in multiple arenas: military coalitions; ideology, psychology, and espionage; sports; military, industrial, and technological developments, including the space race; costly defence spending; a massive conventional and nuclear arms race; and many proxy wars. There was never a direct military engagement between the United States and the Soviet Union, but there was half a century of military build-up as well as political battles for support around the world, including significant involvement of allied and satellite nations in proxy wars.

A **proxy war** is the war that results when two powers use third parties as substitutes for fighting each other directly. While superpowers have sometimes used whole governments as proxies, terrorist groups, mercenaries, or other third parties are more often employed. It is hoped that these groups can strike an opponent without leading to full-scale war.

(Wikipedia definitions of Cold War and proxy war, **en.wikipedia.org**)

Document 3   War on drugs

The **War on Drugs** is a prohibition campaign undertaken by the United States government with the assistance of participating countries, intended to reduce the illegal drug trade — to curb supply and diminish demand for certain psychoactive substances deemed 'harmful or undesirable' by the government. This initiative includes a set of laws and policies that are intended to discourage the production, distribution and consumption of targeted substances. The term was first used by President Richard Nixon in 1972, and his choice of words was probably based on the War on Poverty, announced by President Lyndon Johnson in 1964.

(Wikipedia definition of War on Drugs, **en.wikipedia.org**)

A suitable way of answering the question could be as follows:

> According to Document 1, war should be defined as large-scale armed conflict between nations or large factions. Document 2 uses the word instead to describe a prolonged period of hostility and preparation for conflict, as the Cold War did not entail fighting between the USA and USSR, only the stockpiling of weapons and proxy wars between other nations supported by the superpowers. Document 1 undermines the usage in Document 2, stating: 'The conflict of arms must be actual, and not merely latent, for it to count as war'.

> Document 3 implies a third meaning; organised opposition to a particular threat, as in the wars against drugs and poverty. This usage is also found in Document 1, which refers to the 'war against terrorism'. Problems arise because of inconsistency of use between the three sources, the first predominantly using the word literally and the second and third using it figuratively to describe situations that resemble war in terms of a long struggle against a perceived enemy.

This would be an appropriate length of answer if 6 marks were available. A 4-mark answer would need to be briefer.

2 *Questions of measurement*

A similar low-mark question you might expect is one that asks about difficulties of measuring a particular phenomenon. This is rather like the definition question as it entails deciding how you would recognise the phenomenon in the first place as well as considering how you would measure its extent.

To practise this skill, read the two documents below and then attempt to answer this question:

> What problems might arise in using Document 4 to measure the extent and scale of 'obesity'?

Notice that, even though the question only refers to Document 4, you may be able to use ideas from Document 5 (and other documents on the examination paper) to challenge its suggestions.

Document 4   Medical terms for obesity

Obesity traditionally has been defined as a weight at least 20% above the weight corresponding to the lowest death rate for individuals of a specific height, gender, and age (ideal weight). 20–40% over ideal weight is considered mildly obese; 40–100% over ideal weight is considered moderately obese; and 100% over ideal weight is considered severely, or morbidly, obese.

More recent guidelines for obesity use a measurement called BMI (body mass index) which is the individual's weight multiplied by 703 and then divided by twice the height in inches. BMI of 25.9–29 is considered overweight; BMI over 30 is considered obese. Since the BMI describes the body weight relative to height, it correlates strongly (in adults) with the total body fat content. Some very muscular people may have a high BMI without undue health risks.

(Sourced from the **Answer.com** and **Medicine.Net.com** websites)

Document 5   The National Association to Advance Fat Acceptance

Historically, obesity researchers have sought an answer to the question, 'How can we make fat people thin?' The underlying assumptions are that thinness is more desirable, that fatness increases health risks, that permanent weight loss is possible, and that weight loss increases longevity.

These assumptions run contrary to the experience of most fat people, which is that permanent weight loss is unachievable, that dieting makes them fatter, that many of them are healthy, and that valuing thinness over fatness is a cultural bias.

Obesity researchers' hypotheses often incorporate biases against fat people. They use data from studies of very-low-calorie diets (which demonstrate initial weight loss, followed by weight regain and then early death) to 'prove' that being fat is unhealthy, rather than interpreting the data to mean that very-low-calorie diets are unhealthy.

Obesity researchers refuse to see that fatness is a cultural issue. When they acknowledge the social stigma involved in fatness, they see the solution as changing body size rather than eradicating the stigma.

Most obesity researchers experience an economic conflict of interest. The 1985 National Institute of Health (NIH) conference which proclaimed obesity a 'killer disease' also arbitrarily redefined obesity in such a way as to affect millions more Americans. This redefinition and the call for treatment translated into vastly increased research funding, weight loss industry profits, and physicians' revenues. The chairman of the conference was a paid consultant to United Weight Control and two doctors considered to be leading authorities in obesity research were paid consultants to the makers of Optifast, a low-calorie diet product.

Due to the economic interests and bias of leading obesity researchers, research not supporting weight loss isn't funded and isn't published. Advocates for the fat community are rarely consulted by NIH or by researchers investigating obesity-related issues.

The National Association to Advance Fat Acceptance (NAAFA) believes the primary goal of obesity research should be to improve the health and well being of fat people rather than weight loss. NAAFA condemns those obesity researchers who use their position as public health policymakers to further their own economic interest. NAAFA demands that the NIH fund new investigators and studies focussing on non-dieting alternatives to improve the health and well-being of fat people and that fat people have a voice in the types of weight-related issues being researched and the development of public policy about fatness.

(Extract from **www.naafa.org**)

Here is a possible answer:

> Document 4 presents statistics-based definitions of obesity. These carry a certain amount of authority because they are couched in scientific language, but the account presents almost too much information because criteria are given for three degrees of obesity, mild to severe. The matter is complicated by an alternative measure, the BMI, more up to date but sometimes misleading for very muscular people. It is therefore unclear whether to use the first set of criteria (assuming we also had figures for ideal weights) or the BMI measurements.
>
> Document 5 casts doubt on both these possibilities, radically suggesting that obesity can be 'arbitrarily redefined' by specialists to enrich the diet industry and medical specialists. This suggests the criteria have no scientific basis and reflect cultural bias. Therefore a fundamental problem of using either of the measures of obesity in Document 4 is that these measures may be less objective than they seem, as they could shift according to the whim of professionals with vested interests.

This answer would be more than adequate for 6 marks; you would need to be considerably briefer if only 4 marks were available. A useful rule of thumb is to make one point or write about one meaningful sentence per mark. Examiners report that many candidates write too much for such low-mark questions, neglecting the higher-mark questions as a consequence. For this type of question they reward answers that contain:

- identification of problems of measurement (which might include problems of definition)
- a brief explanation or exploration of the problems
- reference to the documents

As the wording of the question referred to 'problems' (in the plural), the answer above satisfies this by referring to more than one: the complications involved in the scientific measurement in Document 4 and the suggestions in Document 5 that definitions of obesity underlying its measurement could be biased and shifting. The answer above made explicit references to each document and quoted from the second.

Candidates sometimes find it useful to consider problems of definition in terms of the following:

- vagueness
- ambiguity
- context

Consider the use of the term 'obesity' in the document below and decide which of the three types of problem is best illustrated.

Document 6   Treat child obesity as neglect say doctors

Children under 12 should be taken into care if they are obese, according to doctors. The call comes after a survey of paediatricians revealed that obesity was a factor in 20 child protection cases last year. Concerns were raised after a BBC investigation found children as young as 6 months were overweight due to parental overfeeding.

The problem is so widespread that the British Medical Association will debate a motion on childhood obesity at its annual conference. Doctors will say that, in extreme cases, overfeeding a child under 12 should be seen as a form of abuse or neglect and treated as a child protection issue.

Dr Matthew Capehorn, who put forward the motion, said: 'If you are faced with a child who is severely under-nourished, social services, doctors and other authorities would be involved. But the same approach is not taken when faced by a child who is obese. Having a child who is overweight poses as much of a danger to their health as a child who is suffering malnutrition; arguably, even more risk.'

Dr Tabitha Randell, a consultant paediatric endocrinologist at Nottingham University Hospital, claimed some parents are killing their children with kindness. She said: 'I get many parents of obese children claiming there must be a problem with the child's glands causing the weight issues. But this is very rarely the case. Parents seem unable to accept that it is a matter of controlling food intake.'

But the Royal College of Paediatrics and Child Health does not support the conference motion. It said: 'Obesity is a public health problem, not a child protection issue.'

(Extract from **www.thisislondon.co.uk**)

Hopefully you have recognised that the problem here is **vagueness**. Obesity is never defined and the word is used interchangeably with 'being overweight'. This is an everyday use of the term, but it lacks precision and there is no discussion of what counts as overweight. (Views of ideal weights vary greatly between cultures.) If we compare this with Document 4, we find that those who are over 'ideal weight' but by less than 20% are not considered even 'mildly obese' by some scientists, so the two documents are incompatible. Another way of expressing this problem is that the terms 'obesity' and 'being overweight' are **conflated** in Document 6.

 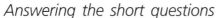

Ambiguity, on the other hand, suggests the possibility of two or more distinct meanings. The phrase 'some parents are killing their children' usually means that murder is occurring, but in Document 6 it is used to suggest adults being unwittingly responsible for a decline in their children's health over a long period, that could eventually lead to premature death. It is worth noting that the phrase is used here as an **appeal to fear**, drawing on the fact that it often carries the other meaning. This is something to comment on when you are invited to critically assess the documents.

Context clearly relates to the definitions of obesity mentioned in Document 5. NAAFA suggests that 'valuing thinness over fatness is a cultural bias' and that those whom professionals regard as obese might not see themselves as having a health problem and are only disadvantaged by the stigma. Context then can relate to issues such as:

- scientific or professional versus everyday usages
- changes in usage over time
- usage in different circumstances
- usage in different countries, religions, ethnic, social and political groups or, as in the NAAFA example, pressure groups. (This relates particularly to cultural relativism: poverty, child neglect, sex abuse, cruelty to animals and many other such terms would be used differently by members of different cultures depending on the degree of poverty and so on that is the norm in their society.)

3 How interpretation differences might affect action

A likely follow-up question to one about definition or measurement might ask:

> Referring to relevant documents, explain how differences in interpretation of the term 'obesity' might affect the implementation of related social policies.

Consider the problems of defining and measuring obesity in the light of this question, reminding yourself of Document 6 above and reading Document 7. What would happen if medical experts and politicians could not agree on the extent of obesity?

Document 7 *Storing up problems: the medical case for a slimmer nation*

'Storing up problems: the medical case for a slimmer nation' produced jointly by the Royal College of Physicians, the Faculty of Public Health, and the Royal College of Paediatrics and Child Health, argues that action needs to be taken at every level — national, local, community and as individuals, together with an understanding of the social and cultural factors that are behind the progressive increase in overweight and obesity.

The report states that actions should be long term and sustainable, recognising that behaviour change is difficult and takes time. The emphasis is on environment, empowerment and encouragement — dropping the blame culture, engaging the whole community and assisting all groups to take action according to their own opportunities and responsibilities, including health professionals themselves.

Over half the UK population is either overweight or obese. One in five adults is obese. Obesity in 2–4 year old children almost doubled from 1989 to 1998, and in 6–15-year-olds trebled between 1990 and 2001. If current trends continue, conservative estimates are that at least one-third of adults, one-fifth of boys and one-third of girls will be obese by 2020.

Being overweight restricts body activity, damages health and shortens life; and it harms self-esteem and social life. Heart disease, stroke, joint problems and the commonest form of diabetes (Type 2) are direct effects. Overweight and obesity also result in a huge financial burden for government, the NHS and society as a whole.

According to Professor Siân Griffiths, President of the Faculty of Public Health, the UK has the lowest physical activity for school children in Europe and we are eating the wrong foods. The solution requires partnerships at all levels, across government, who can regulate and create health policies, and within communities where engagement in healthier environments (such as schools, workplaces) can encourage individuals in making healthier choices.

(Royal College of Physicians News, 11 February 2004, **www.rcplondon.ac.uk**)

The answer to this question seems fairly obvious — if people did not agree about the extent of the problem, they might not take it seriously. However, you would need to answer in more specific detail and make references to likely policies mentioned in the documents to stand a good chance of earning the full 4–6 marks likely to be available for this type of question. Here is a suggested answer:

> Document 6 mentions the very controversial issue of child protection, implying that children might be taken into care and their parents punished for child neglect for 'overfeeding a child under 12'. Clearly it would be impossible to enforce this policy if there was disagreement between authorities about the definition of 'overfeeding', which would relate to definitions of obesity.

> Document 7 admits that 'behaviour change is difficult and takes time' but that 'the whole community' needs to be engaged. This can only be the case if there is a consensus, so that, for example, those in charge of schools and workplaces can spread a consistent message about the need for change. Likewise 'partnerships… across government' will only be achieved if all agree on the scale of the problem and therefore make it a priority, as tackling it will reduce the resources available for other areas of need.

4 *Factors that might affect how people react to a phenomenon*

A similar type of short question could ask you to identify and explain several factors that might affect how people react to the key issue described in the resources. You should usually be able to identify different viewpoints in the various documents. If you can work out what distinguishes the holders of these differing views from each other, then you should be able to arrive at a suitable answer. Now think about the following question, worth 6 marks:

> With reference to relevant documents, identify and briefly explain three factors that might affect how people react to obesity.

Skim-read Documents 4 to 7 again to remind yourself of the different reactions to obesity and the types of people involved. It helps the examiner if you identify the

three factors in separate paragraphs. Begin with a concise identification of the factor and then, in the following sentence or two, explain your answer by referring to those affected by that factor according to a particular document. Here is a possible answer:

> One relevant factor could be whether people have personal experience of obesity. In Document 5 the National Association to Advance Fat Acceptance suggests that many such people are happy with their weight, except for the stigma, whereas health professionals take an outsider's view, biased in favour of thinness.

> Another factor could be information or lack of it. Document 6 describes parents who overfeed their children through ignorance, whereas paediatricians understand the causes of obesity and may regard it as a form of abuse.

> A third factor could be economic. Document 5 suggests some parties may exaggerate the extent and seriousness of obesity to make money from slimming products and treatments. Document 7 predicts that obesity could 'result in a huge financial burden for government, the NHS and society as a whole', implying that taxpayers may soon show more concern.

The other type of low-mark question you are most likely to encounter relates to identifying a dilemma, but this needs to be chosen carefully as it has to be explored more fully in the essay question that follows. As these two related questions are likely to come at the end of the question paper, they will be discussed later. First we shall turn to the long question relating to criteria and choices.

B Answering longer questions

1 Explaining how potential choices are affected by criteria

1.1 Choices

In the Unit 3 examination you are likely to be asked to consider a range of possible responses to a complex ethical problem. This range of choices of action could be presented explicitly on the question paper, perhaps in the form of a **continuum**. This is a list of possibilities of which the first and last item represent two extremes, such as the most liberal and the most punitive, with other suggestions arranged between them in a logical order gradually increasing in harshness. Alternatively different possible policies or courses of action may be embedded within the documents for you to identify and explore as potential choices.

Look back at Documents 4 to 7 on obesity and make a list of the different policies that could be pursued. It is always worth considering the possibility of maintaining the status quo, in other words simply continuing with present policies, or of taking no action at all.

1.2 Criteria to apply

You will then be required to apply appropriate criteria to judge the effectiveness of the different choices of action or discuss how decision makers might do so. The example question on the specimen paper reads as follows:

> Explain how the choices that we could make about using wind farms to generate power are affected by the criteria (such as public opinion) that are used in the decision-making process.

Questions on future exam papers may vary in their wording and precise requirements as the new specification develops.

You should recall from Unit 1 that a criterion is a standard, rule or test upon which a judgement or decision can be based. (Ensure that you use this word of Greek origin correctly. Remember that the singular is criteri**on** and the plural is criteri**a**.) You may be invited to choose criteria, such as cost, public opinion, practicality, human rights and social, political or religious considerations, from a list on the examination paper. Otherwise the question may resemble the one above, suggesting one criterion as an example but expecting you to work out others for yourself from the documents and drawing on your experience of the course. You could look at Unit 3 examination papers from the previous specification on the OCR website to see examples of the sort of criteria that have been applied in the past. Before reading on, think of some criteria that could influence decisions about which the possible policies on obesity you have listed should really be employed.

Some possibilities that you might have thought of are outlined below.

Choices

In the case of responding to the apparent problem of childhood obesity, the following represents a series of choices that could be made:

- Focus on informing the public about the unhealthy properties and effects of some foods on sale.
- Make lessons on healthy eating and cookery compulsory in schools and ask schools and workplaces to promote walking and other exercise.
- Send experts regularly to the homes of obese children to give dietary advice.
- Take obese children into care so that their diets can be monitored daily and make it a criminal offence to allow children in one's care to become obese.
- Increase funding for research into the reasons for obesity, encouraging researchers to consult those who are obese.
- Take no action at all to tackle obesity and campaign to reduce its stigma.

Criteria for choices

In responding to the apparent problem of childhood obesity we need to develop criteria that can be used to help us make choices. Examples may include the following criteria:

- effects on public expenditure
- likely effectiveness in reducing obesity
- human rights
- creation of other problems

The questions you could be asked about these criteria and choices are likely to vary from paper to paper, but in every case you are likely to have to apply at least two criteria to

at least two choices, discussing the extent to which, using those measures of judgement, the choices seem viable.

1.3 Assessing the documents

You must draw explicitly on the information in particular documents to help you, commenting as you go on whether the documents themselves are completely convincing. You should be able to evaluate a wider range of more challenging source material than the brief documents specially written for the AS examinations. From them you need to select appropriate ideas, comments and information to support your reasoning and analysis of complex moral and ethical problems. The source material could take the form of:

- factual information in text form
- definitions
- opinion and argument
- numerical and statistical information
- tables, graphs and other visual presentations, such as scattergraphs and pie charts
- statements from experts and from interested parties, such as religious, environmental, social and political pressure groups

You should be able to identify and evaluate conflicting ideas and arguments within the source material, and explain how the ideas and arguments may be influenced by a range of factors. These might be the social, political, religious or moral views of the writers of the sources, so you could apply the credibility criteria covered in Unit 1, such as bias and vested interest, to discuss how seriously the sources should be taken in the decision-making process.

The evidence and reasoning in the documents also needs to be assessed in terms of its strengths and weaknesses, so consider adequacy, relevance, problems with different types of evidence, such as statistics and data from surveys, flaws in reasoning, appeals to emotion and problems with hypothetical reasoning.

You will not have time to identify and explain large numbers of flaws in the reasoning, and there may be very few obvious ones compared with the documents you encountered in Units 1 and 2. If you feel the evidence is strong, then say so and identify what makes it strong, using credibility criteria such as expertise and neutrality and referring to positive aspects such as sample size. Nevertheless remain alert to the possibility that some of the sources, or sections within them, particularly documents from pressure groups, are less objective, reliable or relevant than others when you are trying to make the decisions required by the questions.

You should try to refer to all or most of the documents to provide examples or evidence to support your answers. As Unit 3 is synoptic, you are expected to draw on skills developed at AS to read these sources critically. Here is a checklist you might find useful:

- It is important to note the source of each document and to comment on its credibility and the credibility of any individuals quoted with respect to the CRAVEN criteria where appropriate.
- When referring to evidence you should mention if it appears to be selective, not fully relevant, internally inconsistent or contradicted by evidence in other documents.

- Survey results may be based on **small, unrepresentative samples.** Statistics may be dated or relate to a slightly different issue or group from the one under discussion.
- Look out for **emotional appeals**, **appeals to history**, **authority** and so on, and for loaded language, especially when unsupported by hard evidence, and assess the material accordingly.
- Comment on the effect of any **flaws** in reasoning, such as *ad hominem* and slippery slope, on the credibility of the documents.
- Mention also the **strengths** of the documents, such as convincing-sounding statistics, detailed evidence from research and the presentation of alternative viewpoints.

Planning your answer

Let us suppose now that the question you have to answer is as follows:

Explain how *two* possible choices we could make about dealing with the problem of obesity could be affected by *two* criteria.
- Where relevant, critically assess the material in the Resource Booklet to inform your answer.
- Evaluate the relevance of each criterion.

This task needs to be done systematically. Before you start writing, reread the resources to decide which of your list of possible choices and criteria to focus on for this question. It is better to select choices that are mentioned or implied in more than one document if possible so that you can refer to most of the documents. At the same time you could annotate the resources in relation to credibility with symbols such as W? for possible weaknesses and S? for strengths.

Decide on the order in which you will tackle the task, either looking at each choice in turn according to each of the criteria or using one criterion at a time to consider the choices. The second option has the advantage of allowing you more easily to assess the **importance** and **relevance** of each criterion as you go, an additional requirement of the question. Whichever approach you prefer, make a plan so that you do not become muddled halfway through.

The examiner needs to know from the start which criteria and choices you have decided to use, so it would be helpful to state this in your opening sentences and then to use subheadings to mark the stages of reasoning. An extremely thorough essay might be organised as follows:

In addressing the problem of obesity I shall be applying the criteria of **likely effectiveness** and **human rights** to the following possible responses:
- Focus on informing the public about the unhealthy properties and effects of foods on sale.
- Take obese children into care so that their diets can be monitored daily and make it a criminal offence to allow children in one's care to become obese.

Likely effectiveness

Document 6 suggests there may be considerable ignorance among parents about the causes of childhood obesity, and so **informing the public about the unhealthy properties of foods** on sale appears to be an essential first step in tackling the problem. The document quotes Dr Tabitha Randell, who has expertise as a consultant in paediatrics, making it quite a credible source. Her observation, 'I get many parents

of obese children claiming there must be a problem with the child's glands causing the weight issues' suggests there may be genuine lack of knowledge, but this is followed by the comment, 'Parents seem unable to accept that it is a matter of controlling food intake.' This implies that parents may be resistant to advice, an impression reinforced by the document as a whole, which describes the grave concern of the British Medical Association.

Document 5 casts doubt on the usefulness of diet information, suggesting that dieting makes obese people fatter and that obesity specialists have vested interests in identifying increasing numbers of obese people and recommending costly treatments and products. Instead it advocates 'non-dieting alternatives to improve the health and well-being of fat people'. However, the document needs to be treated with caution as it expresses the views of a pressure group, uses loaded language and sweeping generalisations ('Obesity researchers **refuse to see**...')

Nevertheless these two documents suggest there could be resistance to public information campaigns about the unhealthy properties and effects of foods from both parents and obese people, casting doubt on the likely effectiveness of this measure.

Taking obese children into care so that their diets can be monitored daily is likely to be more effective in the short term for the individuals concerned, and making it a criminal offence to allow children in one's care to become obese is likely to attract enough publicity to shock parents into thinking more carefully about their children's diets.

However, Document 7 reminds us that 'one in five adults is obese'. Although the problems of defining and measuring obesity might make us cautious about accepting these exact figures, the prevalence of adult obesity is unlikely to be reduced by taking obese children into care, and once those children are old enough to live independently they may slip back into obesity. Therefore for adults, a public health campaign, even if it only persuades a few, is likely to be more effective than measures targeted at children.

Likely effectiveness is a highly relevant criterion as well-intentioned campaigns that are ignored by the majority and measures targeting only a few individuals will waste public money without bringing broad and significant benefits.

Human rights

Human rights are unlikely to be infringed by a **public information campaign**, providing it is sensitive enough not to arouse prejudice against overweight and obese people, as suggested in Document 5 ('biases against fat people'). Document 7 is a fairly convincing source as it comes from the Royal College of Physicians, although it is rather dated (2004). It seems to support greater information to the public, though solutions to obesity are described in rather vague and general terms. According to Professor Siân Griffiths, who should have an expert overview as President of the Faculty of Public Health, 'we are eating the wrong foods' and 'the solution requires partnerships...within communities where engagement in healthier environments (such as schools, workplaces) can encourage individuals in making healthier choices'. 'Empowerment and encouragement — dropping the blame culture' are advocated, suggesting that no one's dignity or freedom will be jeopardised by these voluntary measures.

In contrast people's right to a family life would certainly be threatened by **taking obese children into care**. There would be likely to be so much opposition to this measure that those imposing it would have to present convincing evidence that children were obese (as measured by widely agreed criteria) and that this was because of overfeeding. Proving the latter would involve state intrusions into private life, another human rights issue. As a result many cases would be contested and it is likely that only a very small proportion of overweight children would be taken into care and perhaps only for a short time. Once returned to their families, it is likely that resentment against perceived 'nanny state' interference might result in little attempt to adhere to recommended diets.

Human rights is an important criterion as measures that infringe rights are likely to be resisted by the public, so that they are rarely implemented in practice or, if they are, those who see themselves as victims may seek to undermine them. With this in mind, it is likely that informing the public about the unhealthy properties and effects of foods would be the better choice of policy.

This answer is probably considerably longer than you could manage in the time allowed. It has been provided as an example to allow you to see how documents can be used as evidence and briefly assessed. The essay is organised in a straightforward way using subheadings, and a reference to the relevance or importance of each criterion is made at the end of each section. Though rather obvious, these points were a requirement of this particular question so they need to be made explicitly. Always check over the bullet points to ensure you have done everything the question asks of you.

Realistically you would probably make some but not all of these points. It is important that you practise this type of task in timed conditions to see how much you can manage to write, as you need to allow time to write an even longer essay afterwards. According to the specimen paper, you would have about 30 minutes minus thinking time to answer this 20-mark question, but check to make sure these details are still correct as the question papers may change a little over time.

Your essay in response to this question will be marked according to a set of criteria. To be placed in the top band, your work needs to demonstrate the following qualities:

Criteria for top-level marks
- Sustained, clear and explicit application of the stated number of criteria to the stated number of choices.
- Explicit reference to relevance, usefulness or importance of each criterion as applied to choices.
- All or most of the documents referred to with explicit, accurate and appropriate use of evidence.
- Material critically assessed in terms of utility, credibility, authority, flaws and assumptions where appropriate.
- Very effective, accurate and clearly expressed explanation and reasoning. Well-reasoned, clearly structured discussion or argument with conclusions about each criterion explicitly stated and convincing.
- Grammar, spelling and punctuation very good with few errors if any.

B *Answering longer questions*

Take particular note that written communication is assessed here, hence the need to plan carefully for what is quite a complex task.

It would be useful to make a checklist of possible criteria that could be applied to courses of action relating to a range of different situations in case such a list is not included on the examination paper. Some are likely to be relevant to almost every situation, such as:
- cost
- likely effectiveness
- practicality (ease of implementation)
- creation of new problems (side-effects)

Others may apply to a narrower range of situations and appropriate phrasing may vary:
- human rights
- freedom of choice
- good of the majority
- effects on minority ethnic, religious or social groups
- effects on different age groups/sexes
- effects on wildlife/biodiversity
- effects on the environment
- effects on the workforce
- likely long-term effects, e.g. on future generations
- likely short-term effects
- public opinion (locally or nationally)
- international opinion/likely effects on international relations

Try to add to this list yourself. If the question allows you a free choice of criteria, it can be better to avoid writing about those that are similar to ethical positions, such as 'human rights' and 'freedom of choice' (which reflects the libertarian position), as you may wish to explore these later in the final question. With this in mind, read the whole examination paper and briefly plan all your answers rather than plunging in and then realising that your answers are becoming repetitive. You are unlikely to receive much credit for making very similar points in two answers.

2 Identifying dilemmas

In the Unit 3 examination, it is likely that you will be asked to identify one (or possibly more than one) **dilemma** that arises in making decisions concerning the issue in the question. Later you will have to explore the dilemma in a long essay question, so it is important to plan ahead and choose one that is significant and interesting rather than a trivial one.

A dilemma is a situation in which there are **alternative, mutually exclusive courses of action**, each of which has **undesirable consequences** for some people as well as **benefits for others**. In some cases the rights of a minority may have to be balanced against the wishes of the majority.

It is important to phrase a dilemma clearly and fully enough to obtain the marks available (probably 2) and the question may emphasise this by asking you to 'state and explain' a dilemma. You need to mention:
- the alternative courses of action

- the benefits of each one to people in specific situations or circumstances or perhaps to the majority
- the drawbacks of each one to particular people

Despite covering all these points, you need to avoid writing in a long and rambling way that wastes time. One way to do this is to compose two sentences beginning with the word 'if', each one dealing with a different course of action. Alternatively the word 'whereas' or the phrase 'on the other hand' would usefully link your assessments of the two options.

Consider the example below to decide whether it deserves full marks:

> If we enforce harsh policies against carrying knives, craft workers who use them professionally will be criminalised.

This answer would not be fully rewarded because the writer has not explained who would benefit from the harsh policies against carrying knives, probably assuming that everyone agrees that the general public would be safer. However, this is not obvious enough and so it must be stated explicitly. The writer has only identified a problem, not a dilemma. Consider this second attempt:

> Enforcing harsh policies against carrying knives would probably reduce knife crime, benefiting the general public, but would criminalise craft workers who need them in their work.

This might earn full marks from a generous examiner, but it is not a safe answer as it fails to state the alternative course of action. It is not clear, for example, whether one of the possibilities we are considering is legalising the carrying of knives completely or adopting a more discretionary approach. This final version makes it clear and is thorough enough for full marks while still quite concise:

> Enforcing harsh policies against carrying knives would probably reduce knife crime, but could criminalise craft workers who need them in their work. On the other hand, a policy where more discretion was applied could leave the public in greater danger of knife attacks.

You may think that dilemmas are easy to explain but many students lose marks by assuming that certain points are obvious and failing to make them explicitly. Others waste time by explaining them at unnecessary length. It is therefore important that you obtain plenty of practice in expressing dilemmas in writing, seeking feedback from your teacher that your explanation is detailed and clear enough and yet concise.

3 Attempting to resolve a dilemma

The final question on the examination paper is likely to carry the most marks (30 marks on the OCR specimen paper). It requires you to attempt to resolve the dilemma you have identified by applying ethical principles (that may be derived from ethical theories).

You should recall that an ethical principle is a general rule about what constitutes right or wrong behaviour, such as 'We should treat people as equals'. An ethical theory is a more developed set of moral beliefs generated by philosophers, religious groups or social movements. For example, Communists and Christians both believe in the principle that we should treat people as equals, but the groups have very different and complex

theories about how and why this should be done. The examination question gives you the choice of whether to apply ethical principles or theories or a mixture of both.

This is the part of the course most likely to involve you in a certain amount of reading, checking that you understand and can apply ethical theories to a variety of situations and that you can remember them correctly. Most of your revision for Unit 3 should focus on this area.

3.1 How many ethical theories should you know?

The specification suggests you need to know the difference between **teleological (or consequentialist) theories**, such as utilitarianism, and **deontological theories** such as **duty ethics**. It mentions philosophers such as J. Rawls and J. S. Mill, though the earlier philosophers Kant and Bentham are similarly important. The concepts of altruism and elitism are also mentioned in the list of recommended vocabulary.

It is advisable to be well acquainted with several ethical theories as you are expected to apply at least two and there are occasions when particular theories seem less relevant. Critical thinking writer Roy van den Brink-Budgen suggests that three theories, deontological, consequentialist and right libertarian positions, are likely to be sufficient for dealing with most ethical dilemmas and demonstrates this in his textbook *Critical Thinking for A2* (2006).

The account below covers considerably more and you would be advised to read them and decide which others, besides the three mentioned above, appeal to you. The natural law position, for example, is useful when considering medical and environmental ethics. You may already be well acquainted with left-wing theories, Christian values or human rights from your other studies or life experience.

3.2 Deontological versus teleological theories

Ethical theories or positions are sometimes divided into two groups. Those that try to judge whether acts are intrinsically good, regardless of their final results, are known as **deontological positions** or **duty ethics**. Those that focus on the end result of particular acts are known as **consequentialist** or **teleological** (purpose-orientated) theories.

Before we go into detail, a simple example might help you to see the difference, although it is not always so clear cut. Suppose a loving husband were to burgle a chemist's shop because this was the only way to obtain a large supply of a highly expensive drug which could cure his wife's life-threatening illness. From a duty ethics point of view, this action is unethical, as stealing is intrinsically wrong. To a consequentialist this action could be justifiable as its purpose was to save a life and the chemist's loss is minor in comparison. Now we shall examine duty ethics in more detail.

Deontological theories or duty ethics

Deontological theories focus on whether acts are intrinsically good, regardless of their consequences. The word **deontological** relates to duty, doing what is obligatory or morally upright. The early Greek philosopher Socrates took this line, arguing that actions were good if they adhered to independently valid principles, but this gave rise to the question of how people would recognise and agree on these principles. An answer was suggested much later by Immanuel Kant (1724–1804).

Kant's categorical imperative

Kant, in *Groundwork of the Metaphysic of Morals* (1783), described the **categorical imperative**; the absolute duty to follow general principles of right conduct, ignoring vested interests and possible consequences of the specific action and acting out of **good will**. An 'imperative' is something that must be done (or in some cases must not be done) and by 'categorical' Kant meant that the moral law should be based on pure objective reason about what would be best for mankind in general, not swayed by subjective feelings about what might be the best course of action in particular circumstances.

Kant's theory is well illustrated by considering the activities of police marksmen. There was a long investigation after the Brazilian electrician, Jean Charles de Menezes, was shot in the London underground in 2005. The police who shot him thought he was a terrorist. In 2006 another innocent member of the public, Harry Stanley, was shot dead in the street because police thought a table leg he was carrying in a bag was a shot gun. In each case the police were focusing on the consequences of acting or failing to act. If these men had been criminals with violent intentions, then to stop them in their tracks could have saved many other lives.

In contrast followers of Kant would say that killing is nearly always wrong regardless of the situation. Consequences can never be predicted with certainty, so it is wiser to choose actions that are intrinsically good. Even an armed villain might be talked out of his intended crime, might suddenly suffer a heart attack and be unable to carry out his plan or his bomb might fail to explode. In the cases described above it is clear that taking the deontological approach, not shooting people because it is intrinsically wrong, would have been the better of the two options.

Kant suggested that moral guidelines could be worked out using the **universalisability principle**:

> Act only according to that maxim whereby you can at the same time will that it should become a universal law.

This means people should only act in ways that they would be willing for everyone else to act in any circumstances. Thus lying, even to save a friend, is not acceptable because all the institutions in society will crumble if we can no longer rely on each other's word.

Kant defended this position to a critic by illustrating it with a situation in which a man thought he was saving his friend from a potential murderer by trying to lie that his friend was not at home. Unbeknown to him, the friend had feared the attack and sought refuge in the very place named by the liar. Hence breaking a moral code is never justifiable because consequences can never be predicted and, more fundamentally, because it threatens to disrupt the very basis of our society. In this instance if it was universally acceptable to lie, then no one would believe anyone and all truths would be assumed to be lies. Likewise Kant condemned laziness, suicide and unwillingness to help the needy since a universal adoption of any of these would result in social chaos.

Kant also maintained that other people should be regarded as rational beings with purposes of their own and should not be treated simply as a **means** to our own **ends**. Hence slavery is abhorrent because the master uses the slave for his own purpose with no regard for the person's rights. By the same token unfair trade and exploitation of workers are rejected by modern deontologists. Though he did not view animals as

rational enough to have rights, Kant condemned animal cruelty as it lacked compassion and was likely to degenerate into unsympathetic treatment of fellow human beings. Our moral duty should be to avoid harm to others, respect their autonomy and be as just to them as possible.

You may have noticed the comment above that killing is '*nearly* always wrong'. Perhaps not surprisingly, as he was writing two centuries ago, Kant believed in capital punishment for murderers, following the retributive principle that criminals deserve punishment, and punishment should be equal to the harm done. Likewise robbers deserve having some of their property confiscated. Kant would almost certainly have stopped short of suggesting that those guilty of cruelty should be treated cruelly, as the dignity even of criminals has to be respected, even though they have sacrificed some of their rights to autonomy by taking away the rights of others.

John Rawls and the *Theory of Justice*
The modern philosopher John Rawls followed Kant in believing that there were moral duties that should be followed for the benefit of all humanity. In *The Theory of Justice* (1971) he suggested a thought experiment. Appropriate rules of social justice could be devised if citizens representing several generations could devise the principles in advance without knowing what position they would hold in the society. This **veil of ignorance** would result in a constitution with similar rights for people of all stations and, as all had agreed to it, there should be little dispute once citizens found out the roles they were to play. Each person would have as much liberty as was compatible with that of others. The only inequalities within the society would be ones that everyone agreed were fair, so the society would be stable with little law breaking. Of course Rawls' suggestions could only be carried out to the full if a new human settlement were to be set up, for example on another planet. Nevertheless they provide food for thought.

W. D. Ross and conflicting duties
Ross (1877–1971) modified Kant's theory of absolute duties, suggesting that sometimes there had to be exceptions if duties conflicted. He identified several **prima facie (at first sight) duties** that should be obligatory unless they are overridden by other duties. In other words there is a prima facie duty to act in a certain way, unless moral considerations override this. Our **actual duty** is the duty we should perform in the particular situation. Whatever one's actual duty is, one is morally bound to perform it.

Prima facie duties are as follows:
- **Fidelity**. The duty to keep one's promises and contracts and not to engage in deception.
- **Reparation**. The duty to make up for the injuries one has done to others.
- **Gratitude**. This could include providing help where possible to those who have helped us.
- **Non-injury**. Refraining from doing others harm and making an effort to prevent harm to others from other sources.
- **Beneficence**. Acting for the good of others to foster their health, security, wisdom, moral goodness or happiness.
- **Self-improvement**. To act so as to promote one's own good, i.e. one's own health, security, wisdom, moral goodness and happiness.

Ross's theory is useful in that it acknowledges the importance of personal bonds in specific situations. A strict follower of Kant would be hard pressed to know whether to rescue his own loving parent or a stranger if only one could be saved. According to Ross the rescuer would be justified in prioritising the parent because of the *prima facie* duty of gratitude.

Unfortunately even Ross's theory has some weaknesses. He admitted that his list of duties was incomplete and did not place the duties in order of priority, making it difficult to decide which to follow if there was a conflict between them. His suggestion was that this would be self-evident to mature, intelligent people with deep moral convictions. This, however, is rather a circular argument as, if people already have this sort of moral awareness, there is no need for theories of ethics to provide guiding principles.

3.3 Teleological or consequentialist theories

Teleological theories focus on the end results of actions, judging their morality according to the degree to which their consequences are likely to benefit or harm others. The word teleological is based on the Greek *telos* meaning 'goal'. Jeremy Bentham (1748–1832) argued for the Principle of Utility, developing the consequentialist theory known as **utilitarianism** in the late eighteenth century. His approach was known as 'act utilitarianism', as he attempted to calculate the number of people whose happiness would be affected by a specific act, the extent to which they would be affected and for how long, using the **hedonic calculus**. He treated all the people involved as equals and did not differentiate between different types of pleasure. A modern **act utilitarian** might justify the assassination of President Robert Mugabe, which could potentially save the lives of thousands of Africans.

Problems of adopting a utilitarian approach include determining with any degree of conviction what all the consequences of an action are likely to be. Should we guess at the consequences for future generations? Another issue is how we can measure and compare the different kinds of pleasure or pain various people might experience as a result of a certain act.

In the nineteenth century John Stuart Mill (1806–73) in his book *Utilitarianism* modified Bentham's theory. Instead of calculating the consequences of specific acts, he suggested it was more practical to judge **types of actions**, using rules based on past experience of what would benefit society as a whole. Unlike an act utilitarian interested in the ethics of killing Robert Mugabe, a **rule utilitarian** following Mill would argue that killing leaders or people in general cannot be acceptable. Safeguarding the right to life maximises general happiness far more than condoning murder. Likewise lying and stealing are unethical because, if widespread, they result in public unease. When considering how to act in specific situations, rule utilitarians may adopt one of two approaches:

- **Strong rule utilitarians** adhere to the general rule about what is usually beneficial, regardless of the details of this particular situation. (In this way they are likely to reach very similar judgements to followers of duty ethics, though working from a different starting point, focusing on good consequences rather than what is intrinsically right.)
- **Weak rule utilitarians** take the general rule into consideration but let the benefits and harm likely to arise from this specific act take precedence in their decision making.

Mill also differed from Bentham in distinguishing different types of pleasure. He described some types of happiness, such as intellectual pleasures, as of a higher quality than the immediate indulgence of physical desires. This went some way towards

answering critics who suggested that utilitarianism might encourage pleasurable vices. For example, making alcohol free might at first glance appear justifiable as it would bring instant pleasure to many but, as it would subsequently reduce the higher quality happiness of being in good health, it would not be ethical after all.

The contemporary philosopher Peter Singer advocates **preference utilitarianism** in his book *Practical Ethics* (1979). He argues that the preferences of all parties involved in an issue should be considered, allowing people to say what for them constitutes pleasure or pain, as it can be subjective. This position may be preferable to Mill's rather elitist stance on intellectual pleasures. In addition consideration should be given to the interests of brain-damaged people, animals and others unable to voice their views, though they may not be weighed equally against the preferences of conscious and rational people. This is a more sophisticated approach than Bentham's version of utilitarianism in which the happiness or harm to all was equally rated, though Singer's approach raises new questions about how we decide whether certain groups of people are rational enough to prioritise their preferences.

Prudentialism is a variation of consequentialism as it relies on predictions about the future. It is also known as the **precautionary principle**, claiming that we are entitled to act to avoid a particular negative effect. If a situation looks potentially dangerous, even though there is only a strong possibility of a negative outcome, we should take defensive steps. Attacking a country thought to have weapons of mass destruction before they can be used against us would be defended by prudentialists. Clearly Kant would take a different view, that making war is always wrong as we would not want our country to be attacked and we could never be certain in advance that the country in question was going to use weapons against us. In the case of the recent war against Iraq, the good sense of Kant's position seems clear, but in the Second World War taking a prudentialist approach against the rise of Hitler would probably have been a wiser move. A current worry is whether other nations should intervene before the 'rogue state' of Iran builds nuclear weapons.

3.4 How much detail should you know?

It has been necessary to outline the developments in deontological and teleological approaches to avoid giving the false impression that all followers of these theories have continued to share the views of Kant and Bentham. Some students, especially those already studying philosophy, may now feel confident enough to be able to distinguish, for example, how different types of utilitarians might try to resolve a particular dilemma.

On the other hand you may be feeling rather muddled by the fact that two theories which initially seemed diametrically opposed ended up sounding as if their followers would make similar judgements. With this in mind, you might be wise to focus your revision on types of consequentialism which contrast most strongly with duty ethics. Act utilitarianism and prudentialism (the precautionary principle) are clearly very different from views such as Kant's. This is immediately clear if you consider how supporters of these theories would have justified the actions of police marksmen described earlier.

Examiners do not expect knowledge of ethical positions any more detailed than has been provided here. All you need is what you can usefully apply in the time available to the dilemma being discussed. Moreover summaries of ethical positions without reference to the task in hand will not earn you marks.

3.5 Libertarianism

The priority of libertarians is maximum freedom for the individual to pursue his or her own goals, providing that in doing so others are not harmed. Many well-known libertarians are right wing and American, supporting capitalism and believing that the inequalities that result are inevitable. They believe those who work hard or take risks, for example by setting up businesses, deserve to be more highly rewarded than others, and for the state to attempt to redistribute wealth is misguided. Robert Nozick, in *Anarchy, State and Utopia* (1974) objected strongly to income tax. He reasoned that some people choose to work little and enjoy more leisure. Others prefer to work longer hours, giving up their free time in order to earn more money to buy the goods they wish. Yet these people are forced through income tax to give up a portion of what they earn to those who choose leisure. Thus the hard workers lose out both on leisure and on money, while the idle gain both. Nozick regarded this as theft or a form of slavery, as high taxpayers work part of the week for nothing. He argued instead for a minimal state that simply keeps the peace but leaves citizens to follow their own aspirations as far as possible.

Along similar lines Milton Friedman in *Free to Choose* (1980) co-authored with Rose Friedman, dismissed the drive to equality as unwise. He pointed out that many people object to paying income tax and, once they begin to evade that law, they could be tempted to evade others, leading to a slippery slope of law breaking. Though many sociologists argue that relative poverty leads to crime, some members of the New Right such as Friedman and Friedrich Hayek suggest that crime will always be with us, and that attempts to enhance state provision increase rather than reduce crime.

The argument is that 'welfare-ism' makes people irresponsible as they know that state benefits and social services will look after them and their dependents so they no longer attempt to work, to save, to take responsibility for themselves or to supervise their children. Like Nozick, these New Right thinkers wish to reduce the 'nanny state' to a minimum. They advocate reducing crime by harsh deterrence, target hardening and stiff punishments rather than by redistributing wealth.

Libertarians believe in reducing the number of laws so that only acts that harm others are forbidden. So-called 'victimless offences', such as substance abuse, prostitution and viewing pornography, should not be illegal. Neither should taking personal risks, such as driving without a seatbelt. People should be encouraged to make decisions about how to conduct their own lives, and paring down the number of laws to a minimum gives individuals more practice in making mature choices as well as freeing the police to deal with crimes that harm others.

Examine the following extract from the American Libertarian Party Program on Crime to see how many of the ideas outlined above you can recognise and how they resemble or differ from duty ethics and consequentialist approaches.

> **The Libertarian Party's solution to America's crime problem**
> We're offering this five-point plan for making America's streets safe again:
>
> **Protect victims' rights**
> Protecting the rights and interests of victims should be the basis of our criminal justice

system. Victims should have the right to be present and heard throughout the prosecution of their case. We would make criminals pay restitution to their victims for the damage they've caused.

End prohibition

Drug prohibition does more to make Americans unsafe than any other factor. Just as alcohol prohibition gave us Al Capone and the mafia, drug prohibition has given us the Crips, the Bloods and drive-by shootings. What's more, drug prohibition also inflates the cost of drugs, leading users to steal to support their high priced habits. Finally, nearly one half of all police resources are devoted to stopping drug trafficking, instead of preventing violent crime. By ending drug prohibition Libertarians would double the resources available for crime prevention.

Get tough on real crime

The Libertarian Party is the party of personal responsibility. We believe that anyone who harms another person should be held responsible for that action. Libertarians would dramatically reduce the number of early releases by eliminating their root cause — prison overcrowding. It has been estimated that every drug offender imprisoned results in the release of one violent criminal.

Protect the right to self-defense

We believe that the private ownership of firearms is part of the solution to America's crime epidemic, not part of the problem. Libertarians would repeal restrictions that make it difficult for victims to defend themselves, and end the prosecution of individuals for exercising their rights of self-defense.

Address the root causes of crime

Any society that lets kids grow up dependent on government welfare, attending government schools that fail to teach, and entering an economy where government policy has crushed opportunity, will be a society that breeds criminals. The Libertarian Party would increase employment opportunities by slashing taxes and government red tape. We would also end the welfare system with its culture of dependence and hopelessness. Most important of all, we would promote low-cost private alternatives to the failed government school system.

This Libertarian program would help make America's streets safe again.

(Extract from **www.lp.org**)

The policies of the American Libertarian Party, the next one in size after the Democratic and Republican parties, are encapsulated in its slogan 'Smaller government, lower taxes, more freedom'. You will have noticed that the freedoms sought include the right to take drugs, as this is regarded as a matter of personal choice, and the right to carry guns. It is unlikely that many deontologists and teleologists would share these positions. Ending the welfare system also strikes non-libertarians as harsh. Deontologists would probably argue that it is our duty to support those unable to fend for themselves and teleologists would wish to avoid the likely tragic consequences of such neglect.

3.6 Paternalism

Paternalists disagree with libertarians, believing that less well-educated and immature members of the public will easily be led astray to indulge in self-harming practices unless the law acts as a deterrent. The drugs trade, prostitution and pornography involve exploitation of vulnerable people, especially the young, and are therefore not victimless. If substance abuse leads to accidents or illness, expenses are incurred by emergency and health services funded by the taxpayer and of course there are emotional as well as economic implications for victims' relatives. Despite the libertarians' desire to prioritise the freedom of the individual, many would argue that allowing people to harm themselves is neither moral nor responsible, as 'no man is an island' and what affects one affects many others. The word 'paternalism' derives from the analogy that the state should be like a wise father protecting his children from endangering themselves, although those who object to this approach make a similar but more critical analogy, that of the 'nanny state' that makes us all too risk-averse and dependent.

3.7 Natural Law

The Natural Law position is easy to understand and is a useful one to apply to any issue that seems to be 'going against nature', such as the creation of designer babies. This theory derived from Aristotle, who believed that everything was designed for a particular purpose and that to fulfil that purpose was natural and therefore good. The proper functions of man could be worked out by making parallels with the natural world where, for example, the purpose of a seed is to grow into a plant and animals pair up in order to produce young. The advantage of Natural Law was that it could be applied universally, regardless of the customs of particular societies.

Thomas Aquinas built on these ideas in the thirteenth century, making Natural Law part of Catholic doctrine. God has created man and the natural world, and any acts that are not in harmony with His purpose for us should be avoided. Hence contraception, homosexual acts and other sexual acts that cannot result in pregnancy are regarded as wrong because the purpose of sex is deemed to be the production of offspring.

This particular example reveals some of the problems of Natural Law theory. Many people would argue that sex has other purposes besides childbirth, such as emotional bonding, and that if same sex people are drawn to each other, this must be natural. Non-religious people may dispute the whole notion of a purposeful creation. Even religious believers have difficulty in explaining the purposes of natural disasters and other aspects of human suffering. It is difficult to argue that everything that occurs naturally is for the best. While many people believe that creating GM crops is wrong because it interferes with nature too much, few would say the same about immunising children or controlling malaria-carrying mosquitoes.

Some thinkers have posed a counter-argument to the Natural Law theory. The philosopher Hobbes and the psychiatrist Sigmund Freud both suggested that man's natural behaviour is aggressive, selfish and sexually predatory, and it is the restraints of society that keep us in check and force us to be behave morally. In contrast the American writer Henry David Thoreau (1817–62) in *Walden or Life in the Woods* advocated living simply in the countryside instead of pursuing an urban struggle of 'quiet desperation', striving to earn a living in order to buy unnecessary consumer goods. His example was followed in hippie communes in the 1960s and 1970s and more recently by environmentalists trying to live sustainably by growing organic produce and generating their own power from natural sources.

The Natural Law position is still a popular one in debates about the environment, cloning, use of spare embryos created during fertility treatment, sexual selection and other bioethical controversies. In such discussions you can gain marks by pointing out the difficulties of deciding what types of behaviour are really natural.

3.8 Applying the theories learnt so far

To help you consolidate the theories recently discussed, consider the situation below and decide how to phrase the dilemma concerning 'designer babies'. Then try to resolve it from the point of view of three ethical positions.

> **'Designer baby' gives hope to his ill brother**
>
> A couple banned from creating a test tube 'designer baby' in Britain to help cure their seriously ill 4-year-old son have had a baby boy after treatment in America. Jamie Whitaker was selected from nine embryos to be the best possible tissue match for his brother Charlie. His parents hope to use stem cells from his umbilical cord to treat Charlie's life-threatening blood disease.
>
> Jamie is only the second British baby to undergo 'tissue typing' tests as an embryo. Yesterday's announcement triggered a debate over the ethics of screening embryos for desirable traits, and how far the state should interfere with parental choice. Charlie suffers from diamond blackfan anaemia, a rare blood disorder in which bone marrow produces too few red blood cells. The only cure is a transplant of bone marrow stem cells from a donor with the same immune system cells. Neither of Jamie's parents nor his sister were suitable.
>
> A naturally-conceived sibling has a one-in-four chance of being a match. After giving birth to Emily, the couple wanted to improve the chances by screening embryos created by IVF. Mr Whitaker said: 'We have always wanted four children, so we just combined having more with helping Charlie.' Blood tests over the next few days will reveal whether he is a perfect tissue match. There is a one in 50 chance that Jamie will carry the same disease as his brother.
>
> Psychologists have argued that babies born to provide tissue to transplant may resent their siblings later in life. Jack Scarisbrick, of the anti-abortion charity Life, said: 'It is wrong that of nine human beings created, eight have died. There has been a huge deliberate wastage of human life. No doubt this boy will be very much loved but children should be brought into the world unconditionally and not to serve some other purpose.'
>
> (Extract from '"Designer baby' gives hope to his ill brother' by David Derbyshire,
> *Daily Telegraph*, 20 June 2003, **www.telegraph.co.uk**)

One dilemma is as follows:

> If the creation of designer babies was banned or delayed because of moral qualms, then the lives of sick children would be lost. However, in the course of bringing medical help to these children, the designer babies may be exploited and not feel valued for their own sake.

In selecting ethical positions to apply to the dilemma you have probably decided that followers of Natural Law would oppose the creation of 'designer babies'. They are born through the production in artificial conditions of a series of embryos, each of which is tested for genetic make-up. This theory takes no account of the intention behind the action, only that it is not natural. You might comment that this theory is not relevant to modern society, although it has plenty of supporters.

Perhaps you have also selected consequentialism. If we use Bentham's version, act utilitarianism, we could apply the hedonic calculus and add up the amounts of happiness or displeasure likely to be experienced by those involved in the scenario. Creating a designer baby is likely to save or at least prolong the life of one child and bring relief to the parents and other relatives, as well as a degree of satisfaction to the medical staff involved. The main loser is likely to be the designer baby, who may wonder whether he or she is valued as a person or primarily as a source of spare parts and worry about how many future demands there may be. Family relationships may be tense at times as a result of this, but less so than if a child was dying. Expensive medical procedures like this might also increase taxes, making the public less happy. Nevertheless it seems likely that producing a designer baby would bring more benefits than problems, making it ethical in the eyes of consequentialists.

If you tried to apply duty ethics to this problem you probably struggled. Creating test tube babies and then rejecting those considered unfit for purpose is so far removed from traditional morality that it would be difficult to apply Kant's theory. If such a thing had been possible in his day, he might have said (and this of course is dangerous hypothetical reasoning about an event that did not happen) that treating a designer baby as a source of spare parts was exploitation. Other people should be regarded as rational beings with purposes of their own and should not be treated simply as a means to our own ends. However, parents in this situation have argued that they wanted another baby anyway, for its own sake, but preferred to be able to select one that could save an older child's life. How would Kant have felt about using someone as a means to a life-saving act *as well as* valuing him or her as an autonomous individual?

Let us consider a more recent branch of deontology as W. D. Ross's ideas about conflicting duties could be a more fruitful starting point for discussion. He identified beneficence as an important moral duty and the parents of the sick child, by seeking a designer baby, are 'acting for the good of others to foster their health'. On the other hand the duty of non-injury, refraining from doing others harm, does not sit well with the destruction of all the embryos that are poor matches. A lot hinges on whether we regard embryos at such an early stage of development as people. Can they be described as **moral patients**, individuals capable of fully understanding what is being done to them and therefore of experiencing suffering? Ross's theory is therefore difficult to apply, especially as he does not indicate which of these duties should take precedence.

In the examination it is quite acceptable to try to apply a theory to the dilemma and eventually point out that its stance on the matter is not clear. If done well, this can show impressive skills of assessment. However, there can be times when you are uncertain about how to apply a particular theory and then you will be pleased if you have learnt quite a few. Supposing you were not confident about applying deontological theories to the designer baby dilemma, would libertarianism be relevant?

Libertarians prioritise choice, believing that people should have freedom to do as they wish, so long as they do not harm others. The state should not interfere in personal matters. Leaving aside what is probably a minority view, that the discarded embryos are potential people who will be harmed, allowing couples to select a baby seems to accord with libertarian ethics. However, they would almost certainly draw a line at continued medical interference with the designer baby. While taking blood from the umbilical cord would be acceptable, more intrusive surgery such as the taking of a kidney before the child was old enough to give informed consent would be an infringement of the individual's rights.

We could conclude therefore that, although followers of natural law would disagree with the creation of designer babies, consequentialists would be likely to support it. Libertarians too would support the parents' right to choose this, but, despite wanting to keep legislation to a minimum, might suggest safeguards protecting the designer baby's own rights.

Having gained experience in applying these ethical theories, you should now be ready to read about a few more. The human rights position is one we hear frequently mentioned in the news.

3.9 The social contract and human rights

A number of philosophers have disagreed strongly with the view that 'natural' behaviour is good. Plato argued in *The Republic* that most ordinary people are naturally selfish and irrational. When groups of people live alongside each other, there would be anarchy with everyone pursuing their own ends unless a ruler took charge and established principles of right or wrong to which people were expected to adhere.

The British philosopher Thomas Hobbes (1588–1679) agreed, describing life in its natural state as 'nasty, brutish and short'. The powerful would soon overcome the weak, but even the powerful would live in fear of some day being overwhelmed by others. In order to achieve a measure of security, people needed to give up a certain amount of personal freedom. The state would impose laws safeguarding certain **rights** for its members, but in exchange they must take **responsibility** for upholding these laws and expect punishment if they were broken.

These ideas were extended by the philosopher John Locke (1632–1704) in *Two Treatises on Government,* which described the need for rules to be established as populations multiplied and began to compete for scarce land and resources. While in a small settlement individuals had the right to punish those who offended against them, in more complex societies it made better administrative sense for the public to delegate this function to certain officers. However, the powers of authority figures in the criminal justice system and government should be limited and amenable to change by the public who elected them. Locke believed every citizen should have the rights to freedom of speech, religious conscience and property ownership and that it was the duty of the government to uphold these rights.

Philosopher Jean-Jacques Rousseau clarified the issue in his book *The Social Contract* (1762). He said that by entering into this agreement man lost his **natural liberty** and freedom to acquire whatever he could for himself by sheer power. However, he gained **civil liberty**, public recognition that he was entitled to keep his own acknowledged property without others interfering with it. This left him free to get on with other aspects of life instead of constantly having to defend his own property and safety, as the castle builders of the past had to do. The term 'civil liberties' has a similar meaning to **'human rights'**.

There has been considerable debate about how binding a social contract should be, as people have no choice about the country into which they are born and do not actually sign a contract. Some people advocate civil disobedience, the right to act against the law if they feel it breaches fundamental human rights. In 2005, retired vicar Alfred Ridley was sent to prison because he refused to pay his full council tax bill, which he said was unreasonably high. He told the court: 'I am saying that I am not going to pay an illegal council tax demand. No one should pay an illegal council tax demand.'

There is also the difficult issue of how we define **moral agents**. These are rational individuals capable of thinking about and planning actions and they are therefore held responsible for the resulting benefit or harm to others. Are children and the mentally ill or handicapped to be punished for not keeping to the social contract?

In 2007, student Seung-Hui Cho killed 32 people and then himself in a shooting rampage at Virginia Tech. Had he lived, it is doubtful that he would have been charged for murder, because he had earlier been diagnosed as mentally ill. In 2005 Virginia Special Justice Paul Barnett certified in an order that Cho 'presented an imminent danger to himself as a result of mental illness', but recommended treatment for Cho as an outpatient, meaning that he was still at liberty and free to buy guns under American law. This raises the question of whether someone's human rights can reasonably be suspended if they cannot be held responsible for their actions.

A more recent issue is the human rights of terrorist suspects. Here the discussion relates to people who are moral agents and should therefore not be imprisoned without a definite charge being made, which is not possible without substantial evidence. The Habeas Corpus Act of 1679 guaranteed this right in law, although its origins go back much further, probably to Anglo-Saxon times. However, recent highly contested legislation has sought to extend the period for which suspects can be held to 42 days. This raises the question whether the rights of a few individuals, who may be innocent, should be sacrificed for the greater safety of the rest of the population.

Likewise in the case of moral patients, should people in irreversible comas, the mentally ill or handicapped, unborn babies and children be accorded the same human rights as rational adults? In 1990 a legal decision was made to allow a 36-year-old female inpatient at a mental hospital to be sterilised because it was deemed in her best interests by her carers, even though she did not have the mental capacity to give consent to the operation herself.

This type of debate has even extended to the rights of the dead. Dianne Blood's husband, Stephen, contracted meningitis and lapsed into a coma. Samples of his sperm were collected for later artificial insemination and he died shortly afterwards. The Human Fertilisation and Embryology Authority (HFEA) refused to give consent for Mrs Blood to use the sperm to have her husband's baby because he had not given written consent. You could make a link with Kant here, as the court was suggesting that Mr Blood was being exploited as a means to someone else's end.

However, under European law, Mrs Blood had the right to receive medical treatment in another member state, and the HFEA eventually had to let her use the sperm in a Belgium clinic. Subsequently she gave birth to two sons, Liam and Joel, by this method.

This case shows that there can often be conflict between the rights of different individuals in the same case. Some people also argue for the right of children to have a father, which would have complicated the Blood case even more. However, this controversial idea, which discriminates against gay couples seeking fertility treatment or adoption, has not been accepted as an established human right and is unlikely to be so in the foreseeable future.

International human rights agreements

Human rights are debated as part of an ongoing struggle between different pressure groups and interests. In the UK, the welfare state was founded in the mid-twentieth century based on the principle of every citizen's entitlement to certain rights 'from the cradle to the grave', and that the state should supply essentials where the individual was unable to afford them. Housing, healthcare, education, income support and a range of social services were made available to the general public.

In 1948 the Universal Declaration of Human Rights was agreed by the United Nations General Assembly. This is a statement of principles that governments around the world are urged to uphold. As well as enshrining the rights to education, health, shelter and social security established by the welfare state in the UK, other requirements included the following:

- the right to life
- freedom from discrimination
- the right for everyone to be treated equally by the law
- privacy in the home, family and private correspondence
- freedom of expression, association and assembly (the right to gather in groups)
- freedom of thought, conscience and religion
- the right to property
- the right to vote and take part in government
- freedom from torture and cruel or degrading treatment or punishment
- freedom from arbitrary arrest or detention
- the right to a fair trial

Try to remember the above list as these rights are relevant to many contemporary dilemmas. In 1950 the Council of Europe confirmed their intention to 'take the first steps for the collective enforcement of certain of the Rights stated in the Universal Declaration'. These are elaborated in the European Convention of Human Rights. It is worth looking at this in some detail as the names of the rights can be quite misleading; for example, 'right to an effective remedy' is not to do with healthcare but the right to seek redress if any of one's rights have been violated. The right to the peaceful enjoyment of one's possessions is an interesting one as it can be used to protest against new developments such as wind farms or airports that might disturb local residents' peace.

We frequently hear of citizens taking their cases to the European Court of Human Rights because they are dissatisfied with how a court in their own country has dealt with an **ethical dilemma**. Sometimes they may be arguing that, by upholding the rights of an opponent, the law has deprived them of their human rights.

For more details of human rights legislation see the following and similar websites:
- Universal Declaration of Human Rights 1948: **www.un.org/Overview/rights.html**
- Human Rights Act 1998: **www.opsi.gov.uk/ACTS/acts1998/ukpga_19980042_en_1**
- European Convention on Human Rights: **en.wikipedia.org/wiki/European_Convention_on_Human_Rights**

3.10 Egalitarianism and left-wing theories

You may wish to include political theories among the ethical positions you apply to dilemmas, especially if you are already familiar with these from your other studies. Egalitarians believe all people are of equal worth and should be treated the same or equally. They believe that all individuals, regardless of social class, ethnicity, gender or other characteristics, deserve equal opportunities for advancement and an equal share of resources.

The political term **left wing** is used to describe those whose priority is the achievement of social equality **collectively** as opposed to seeking the human rights of individuals. Moderate left-wingers, sometimes called **socialists**, believe in making gradual adjustments to achieve equality, for example by offering the poor free education, training and medical care, taxing high earners and increasing benefits to poorer people, perhaps by topping up low wages.

Marxists take a more radical line on how to bring about social equality. Karl Marx (1818–83) wrote *The Communist Manifesto* with Engels in 1847 and *Capital* in 1867 in which he described Western societies at that time as being dominated by capitalists or bourgeoisie, wealthy owners of land and businesses. These people exploited their workers, the proletariat, and influenced them to accept this as a natural state of affairs. Marxists believe so strongly in equality that they wish to abolish capitalism, closing private businesses and putting all means of production, such as factories and land, in the hands of the state. Workers at state-run collectives would share the profits equally instead of receiving relatively poor wages from the entrepreneur owners. As capitalists would be unwilling to surrender their advantages, this could only be achieved by a revolution.

3.11 Egoism and right-wing theories

The theories above have tended to focus on the individual's role within society, but from earliest times some philosophers have focused on the individual's duty to him or herself. Sometimes this is accompanied by a right-wing lack of regard for the disadvantaged, as we saw in right libertarianism.

Egoism

Ethical egoism maintains that each person ought to maximise their own long-term wellbeing. Their only obligation is to pursue their own self-interest. This position is not advocating self-indulgence, such as getting drunk every day, nor treating others harshly, because in the long term these actions are likely to bring negative consequences to the person concerned. Epicurus was a famous egoist who lived a simple quiet life, believing that long-term pleasure could best be obtained by contemplation of the beauty of art and ideas.

Friedrich Nietzsche, writing in the nineteenth century, stressed the need for personal development and competition, encouraging people to 'rise above the herd' and assert themselves as individuals instead of being cowed by their masters. He despised the 'slave mentality' of democracy and Christianity and asserted that 'God is dead', meaning that people should act according to their own values instead of being inhibited by a God-given morality. He argued in *Beyond Good and Evil* (1886) that 'every morality is a rationalisation of fear', and that people restrained their desires because they expected to be rewarded in the next world, whereas they should take courage and live for the moment. The *Übermensch* or superman, the person with the ability and will to throw off tradition, should pursue his own personal development according to his own values and be master of his own fate.

Elitism

Elitists believe that societies need highly talented people to take the lead. There should be equal opportunities to enable all those with potential to fulfil themselves, and competition should be fair, not based on social origin. However, once selected by merito-cratic processes, talented people may justifiably receive longer and more specialist training than the mass of the population and are likely to acquire more status and higher pay for their responsibilities. Elitists are likely to oppose attempts to 'reduce everyone to the same level' such as the replacement of grammar and secondary modern schools

(for students who respectively passed and failed the 11 plus examination) with comprehensive schools for students of all academic abilities.

3.12 Religious ethics

All religions have their own sets of ethics and some have very useful things to say about humankind's relationship with the environment, bioethics and other issues. If you are fully familiar with the views of a particular religion on an ethical dilemma identified on the examination paper, you are encouraged to discuss it, so long as you balance it with a good variety of alternative ethical positions and maintain objectivity. Most religious faiths are in line with Kant's views to a considerable extent. They advocate **altruism**, the belief that individuals should consider the good of others and act in their interests, as opposed to making their own long-term good a priority (egoism).

3.13 Other ethical principles

In addition to the fully developed ethical theories discussed above, there are ethical principles such as fairness, need and desert which can be applied if you have not already used them as criteria. There is generally less to say about these but referring to a relevant one might sometimes be useful to amplify an answer.

You will have realised by now that knowing a good range of ethical theories has the advantage of allowing more choice when it comes to applying them to a dilemma. If the previous question involved the application of the criteria of 'human rights' or 'fairness' to a series of choices, a candidate who could only think of the human rights or egalitarian positions to resolve the dilemma would have to repeat a considerable number of ideas. In contrast a student able to draw on some quite different ethical positions, such as Natural Law and elitism, could score better marks by making more new points.

Nevertheless you may need to be selective about which of the ethical theories described above you wish to concentrate on when revising. It would be a good idea to look at past papers from the previous specification and discussions in critical thinking textbooks to see the range of dilemmas that have arisen. Then consider which ethical positions you think would be the most appropriate to apply to them and make your own notes to help you to understand and remember them.

3.14 How to tackle the question

The wording of the final question on the Unit 3 paper is likely to be something like this:

> Write an argument that attempts to resolve the dilemma that you have identified. In your argument you should:
> - Identify and use relevant principles (these may be derived from ethical theories).
> - Assess the extent to which these principles/theories are helpful in terms of resolving the dilemma.
> - Use the evidence in the Resource Booklet to support your argument.
>
> *(30 marks)*

Your work will be assigned a level by the examiner, who will be looking for a coherently argued essay demonstrating good skills of communication (AO3) as well as understanding and analysis. Clearly you should be aiming to demonstrate the Level 4 skills set out below and avoid the weaknesses of the lower levels.

Criteria for top-level marks
- There is a sustained and very effective treatment of a clearly understood and relevant dilemma.
- A number of relevant principles are clearly and accurately identified and explained.
- The principles are applied and discussed in a critical manner with clear regard for their relative usefulness in resolving the dilemma identified.
- Evidence from the documents is used to support explanation and argument where appropriate, with clear evidence of discrimination concerning its credibility and relevance.
- The argument attempting to resolve the dilemma is sustained, coherent and convincing throughout, handling some complex material confidently. It is well organised and constructed to enable the reader to follow the reasoning clearly. The argument is likely to include most if not all of the following: reasons, explanations, supporting evidence, counter-argument, hypothetical reasoning, intermediate conclusions and a clearly stated conclusion.
- Grammar, spelling and punctuation are very good. Errors are few, if any.

For practice, read the documents below and jot down possible answers to the following questions. After identifying a dilemma, take some time to think of three ethical theories that you could apply. If this is problematical, consider whether there is a slightly different dilemma that would work better. It can be useful to choose two theories that have points in their favour but disadvantages as well, giving you plenty to discuss, and one that produces a clearer solution or near-solution to the dilemma, enabling you to settle on that one for your conclusion.

(a) State and explain one dilemma that arises in making decisions about safeguarding the nation's health.
(b) Write an argument that attempts to resolve the dilemma that you have identified. In your argument you should:
- Identify and use relevant principles (these may be derived from ethical theories).
- Assess the extent to which these principles/theories are helpful in terms of resolving the dilemma.
- Use the evidence in the Resource Booklet to support your argument.

(30 marks)

Document 1   Folic acid in bread to cut birth defects

Folic acid will be added to bread within a year to reduce the number of babies born with spina bifida and other defects. It will be the first time since the Second World War that food manufacturers have been ordered to add nutrients to improve the nation's health. Experts believe that the compulsory addition of folic acid will reduce the number of cases of spina bifida and other defects by 40%. The vitamin also reduces miscarriages and may help to combat strokes, heart disease and bone disorders in adults.

The decision will raise concerns from some consumers at the erosion of personal freedoms. Compulsory addition of folic acid was ruled out by the Food Standards Agency 4 years ago because medical experts feared that it would mask a vitamin deficiency in the elderly. However, adding folic acid will lessen the 200 cases of babies born each year with spina bifida or other neural tube defects. It will also relieve the distress of up to 750 women a year who have an abortion after discovering that their baby may be born with neural tube defects.

The Agency's advisory committee estimates that if flour were fortified with folic acid at levels of between 100 and 450 micrograms per 100 grams, the number of pregnancies affected by neural tube defects would fall by between 40 and 370 a year. The committee said it now favours compulsory addition of folic acid provided that GPs can monitor the scale of B12 deficiency in elderly patients. Lack of it can trigger anaemia and damage to the nervous system.

Women thinking of becoming pregnant are already advised to take folic acid supplements and to eat foods such as broccoli, Brussel sprouts, beans and peas, which are rich in the vitamin. But half of all pregnancies are unplanned, and the women most at risk are those from poor income groups who are less likely to take vitamins out of ignorance or forget-fulness.

(Extract from 'Folic acid in bread to cut birth defects' by Valerie Elliott,
The Times, 5 April 2006, **www.timesonline.co.uk**)

Document 2 Folic acid might help to combat Alzheimer's

The risk of developing Alzheimer's might be lowered by the consumption of a higher level of folic acid through diet and supplements. Researchers at Columbia University Medical Centre looked over 6 years at the diet and progress of 965 healthy people who had an average age of 75. Around one in five, 192, developed Alzheimer's disease — but those with the highest intake of folic acid had the lowest risk. The recommended daily dose of folic acid is 400 micrograms (0.4 mg) but the average intake in the UK is around 0.2 mg.

Dr Jose Luchsinger, who led the study, cautioned: 'The findings of this study are in contrast to those of some other research. The decision to increase folate intake to prevent Alzheimer's disease should await clinical trials.' Dementia affects over 700,000 Britons, with 500 new cases diagnosed every day as more people live longer.

(Extract from 'Folic acid might help to combat Alzheimer's' by Jenny Hope,
Daily Mail, 8 January 2007, **www.dailymail.co.uk**)

Document 3 Breast cancer fear for pregnant women over folic acid tablets

Taking large amounts of folic acid during pregnancy may increase the risk of breast cancer, a study has suggested. The finding will alarm many women, who are advised by the Department of Health to take folate tablets to protect against having a baby with spina bifida. Doctors were quick to reassure women yesterday, saying that the study results could be a chance finding, were not statistically significant and applied to levels of folate much higher than those recommended by the Department of Health.

The new data comes from the long-term follow-up of nearly 3,000 women who took part in a trial of folate supplementation in 1966–67. They were divided into three groups and given either 5 mg or 0.2 mg folate tablets or a placebo. A team led by Dr Andy Ness of Bristol University has followed up the women nearly 30 years later. In the *British Medical Journal*, they report that 210 of the women have died over this period, and that more of those taking folate, especially at the higher rate, have died than those who took the placebo. The strongest links were seen for breast cancer, where death rates for those on 5 mg folate were twice as high as those on placebo. There were, however, only six deaths in this category, which means that the results are not statistically significant.

In a commentary in the *British Medical Journal*, two US doctors say that other evidence suggests that folate supplementation reduces the risks of breast cancer, especially in women who drink alcohol. Godfrey Oakley and Jack Mandel say that the finding should not deter the fortification of flour with folic acid, which has reduced both birth defects and deaths from heart attacks and strokes in the US.

(Extract from 'Breast cancer fear for pregnant women over folic acid tablets' by Nigel Hawkes, *The Times*, 10 December 2004, **www.timesonline.co.uk**)

Document 4 Institute of Food Research, news release

'Fortifying UK flour with folic acid would reduce the incidence of neural tube defects', said Dr Siân Astley of the Institute of Food Research. 'However, with doses of half the amount being proposed for fortification in the UK, the liver becomes saturated and unmetabolised folic acid floats around the blood stream.

'This can cause problems for people being treated for leukaemia and arthritis, women being treated for ectopic pregnancies, men with a family history of bowel cancer, people with blocked arteries being treated with a stent and elderly people with poor vitamin B status. For women undergoing in-vitro fertilisation, it can also increase the likelihood of conceiving multiple embryos, with all the associated risks for the mother and babies.

'It could take 20 years for any potential harmful effects of unmetabolised folic acid to become apparent.'

It has already been shown that folic acid fortification can exhibit Jekyll and Hyde characteristics, providing protection in some people while causing harm to others. For example, studies have confirmed that unmetabolised folic acid accelerates cognitive decline in the elderly with low vitamin B12 status, while those with normal vitamin B12 status may be protected against cognitive impairment. Around 20% of over 65s in the UK have low B12 status.

Similarly, dietary folates have a protective effect against cancer, but folic acid supplementation may increase the incidence of bowel cancer. It may also increase the incidence of breast cancer in postmenopausal women.

Dr Astley suggests that the use of folic acid in fortification even at low doses could lead to over-consumption of folic acid with its inherent risks.

(**www.ifr.ac.uk**)

Before reading on, check over the notes you have made and compare them with the Level 4 criteria. For example, did you refer to virtually all the documents? Did you briefly assess their credibility? Was your argument organised using appropriate components such as intermediate conclusions?

Now you can compare your notes with the specimen essay below that is attempting to answer the same questions.

(a) If we attempt to reduce the risk of neural tube defects in fetuses by fortifying bread or flour with folates, we risk increasing health problems in some other groups. If we desist from fortification, significant numbers of babies will be born with these deficiencies and many more will be aborted because of this condition.

(b) Paternalism

In addressing this dilemma, paternalists would in principle be in favour of government intervention to improve public health. They would note that it is not always possible for people to make the best dietary decisions for themselves, so those with specialist knowledge have a duty to ensure that the food they access is beneficial.

Document 1 suggests that half the country's pregnancies are unplanned and many women therefore fail to take the folic acid supplements that could reduce the risk of neural tube defects in their babies. Quite a high proportion of those who have unplanned pregnancies could be under-age girls, who fail to make dietary provision for their baby through 'ignorance' so the government has a particular duty of care to them. Unborn babies are the most vulnerable group of all and will suffer most directly if their mothers' diets lack folic acid, <u>so it is only right for the authorities to take control of the issue by fortifying bread</u>, a substance that pregnant women are highly likely to eat every day.

All four documents are likely to contain reliable information. *The Times* has a high reputation for accuracy and the Institute of Food Research is an organisation with relevant expertise. The *Daily Mail* is a more popular paper than *The Times* and needs to be interpreted with caution when expressing views on political issues such as asylum seekers, but its article here appears to be balanced and objective. The scientific evidence mentioned in each source is clearly based on research by named organisations using large samples and it is backed by authoritative sounding statistics. There is a consensus on the beneficial effects of folic acid in early pregnancy on the unborn child. <u>So far the paternalist line seems to provide a clear view suggesting the benefits of fortifying bread or flour with folates.</u>

Prudentialism

Prudentialists would be likely to support the paternalist stance. Following the precautionary principle, the government should be entitled to introduce fortification of foods with folic acid to minimise the incidence of neural tube defects.

However, the problem of taking this line is that if fortification becomes mandatory, then others are likely to be harmed. While Document 2 suggests the supplement may reduce the incidence of Alzheimer's, the other three documents suggest it could increase risks to other groups, including elderly patients with B12 vitamin deficiency. Decision makers have almost as much of a duty to protect the elderly and other vulnerable groups, many of whom will not be aware of the effects of folic acid, as they have to safeguard unborn children. Prudentialists would be unlikely to favour a precaution that protected some groups but increased risks to others. <u>On balance, this makes the paternalist and prudentialist positions less useful for resolving the dilemma than first appeared.</u>

We shall break off from the essay to assess it so far.

The dilemma in question (a) was well chosen so that the essay (question (b)) is relevant to it.

The ethical theories are identified clearly and emphasised by the use of subheadings.

They are explained in just enough detail to show their relevance to the dilemma. The writer has not felt impelled to write everything he or she knows about these theories.

The theories are discussed in a critical manner. Their usefulness is explored at the beginning of the essay, but then the final paragraph reveals the problems of applying paternalism and prudentialism. This prepares the way for an examination of other theories, so their relative usefulness can be assessed.

Evidence from all four documents is used to support the discussion. The credibility of the documents is discussed (emphasised for you in bold at the beginning of the third paragraph).

The argument is well organised in paragraphs. It makes use of reasons, explanations and supporting evidence. There is a counter-argument and hypothetical reasoning, both contained in the same sentence, identified for you in bold, at the beginning of the final paragraph. There are several intermediate conclusions marking the logical reasoning process. These are underlined to help you find them.

Now read on through the rest of the essay to check that its attempt to resolve the dilemma is sustained and that it reaches a clearly stated conclusion.

Act utilitarianism

Consequentialism is another relevant approach to the dilemma, specifically act utilitarianism. We could attempt to apply Bentham's hedonic calculus to work out the amount of benefit or harm likely to occur to different groups if bread or flour is fortified.

Document 1 tells us that 200 children are born with serious disabilities each year and up to 750 more are aborted. Document 2 suggests there could be a reduced risk of developing Alzheimer's for those people who take the recommended dose of folic acid supplement.

On the other side, according to the research described in Document 3, the breast cancer death rate in women who took the high dose supplements was twice as high as those who took none, although researchers suggest the results may have been reached by chance and further investigation is needed. Document 4 refers to a large number of conditions that may be made worse by the supplements. Figures

are only provided for the over 65s, suggesting around 20% of over 65s in the UK with low B12 status could be adversely affected.

It is not practical to carry out a calculation because the only group for which we have fairly reliable numbers is the children in Document 1. We do not know the size of the groups to which the percentages relate or have any figures at all for most of the conditions referred to in Document 4. Even if we had accurate statistics, we would be faced with the impossible task of deciding whether a child born with a disability suffered a greater or lesser degree of harm than a mother dying or an elderly person suffering from 'irreversible damage to the nervous system'. Document 1 also reminds us that the health of the individuals concerned is not the only consideration, as there are the emotional effects on those around them. The issue is further complicated by cost implications. Adding vitamins to bread would be likely to increase the cost to the consumer. Any intervention that changed the incidence of a range of medical conditions would have a complex impact on NHS expenditure and hence on the taxpayer. Act utilitarianism therefore has failed to resolve the dilemma.

Libertarianism

Libertarians would be likely to oppose the mandatory fortification of bread or flour because it takes away the public right to choose ('erosion of personal freedoms', Document 1). Moreover such intervention would probably increase the price of these products that almost everyone needs, instead of giving people the option of spending their money on dietary supplements if they so wish.

In the free market situation that libertarians favour, entrepreneurs in the food industry could fortify some brands of bread and flour and market them at the groups likely to benefit, such as teenage girls, while producing other unfortified brands for the general public. Alternatively, to avoid the problem of family members with different needs sharing the same loaf, folic acid supplements in tablet form could be advertised much more persuasively than they are now to the relevant groups. This would be done by the manufacturers themselves, driven by the profit motive, rather than by the government, avoiding the public's tendency to resist suggestions from the 'nanny state'. While this voluntary approach has the disadvantage that some of those who become accidentally pregnant or who are at risk from Alzheimer's might still not take the supplement, this is more than offset by the fact that none of those for whom folic acid could be harmful are likely to take it. The government cannot be held responsible for damaging some people's health by meddling in their lives.

Conclusion

In conclusion, the libertarian approach seems to offer the most ethical solution to this dilemma. The government should desist from mandatory fortification of flour or bread, leaving the way free for entrepreneurs to target supplements at the appropriate groups and for the public to make their own choices.

Hopefully you agree that this essay is worthy of Level 4. In fact, it has been made especially thorough to offer guidance on how to apply the principles and use the documents and it may be considerably longer than you could write in the allotted time.

A good essay should apply at least two ethical principles in detail and a third perhaps more briefly, as prudentialism is used here. It would be possible to omit one of the theories, such as act utilitarianism, and still earn a high mark.

The essay applying principles to resolve a dilemma needs to be accomplished successfully as it may be worth half the marks of the entire unit. Here is some final advice, drawing together what has already been said.

3.15 Checklist

- Candidates tend to do the last question on the paper least well as they run out of time. There is a tendency to spend too long on the low-mark questions. Read and plan your answers to the whole paper in order, but then consider answering this question and the dilemma-identifying question that precedes it early on, tackling the low-mark questions later. *Providing you number your questions clearly*, the examiner will not object to your answering questions in a different order.
- Make sure you have explained which dilemma you have chosen. (The previous question may have invited you to suggest more than one.) Check that it is one that is relevant enough to the content of the documents and that you can think of at least two ethical principles that could be applied to it with fairly different results.
- Ensure that you have read enough about the ethical theories to be able to apply them appropriately and that you remember their names.
- Try to think of some counter-arguments within the application of each theory. These may arise when the principle is applied to different groups of people mentioned in the documents. Alternatively you may discuss how different philosophers' application of the theory, such as act versus rule utilitarianism or Kant and Ross's versions of duty ethics, could result in a different conclusion.
- Make sure you explain the relevance of each principle you apply to this dilemma. Do not try to show off what you have revised by describing parts of ethical theories that do not relate to the dilemma; this simply wastes valuable time.
- Think how you will organise your essay into paragraphs. You may also wish to use subheadings for each principle and for your conclusion.
- Try to use most of the documents as evidence at some point in the essay. This means forward planning so that you do not repeat evidence and neglect other parts.
- Do not use the documents uncritically. Remember to briefly assess their sources and the credibility of their evidence, but avoid repeating criticisms made in the previous long question. Demonstrate your knowledge by using specialist terminology such as 'expertise' and 'argument by analogy'.
- Try to incorporate hypothetical reasoning, using phrases such as 'If…then…might happen'.
- Conclude each section in which you have applied a principle with an intermediate conclusion in which you assess its usefulness in resolving the dilemma.
- Complete the essay with your assessment of which ethical principle was the most useful, acknowledging any difficulties that may arise in resolving the dilemma.
- Ensure that you know the correct spellings of frequently used words such as 'criterion' and 'principle'. Try to allow time to check over your work for errors of spelling, punctuation and grammar.

C Revision checklist for Unit 3

1 *The examination*

Mark allocation

60 marks, 25% of the total Advanced GCE marks. The paper is not divided into distinct sections. Answer all the questions, some of which will require short answers and some essays. This is a synoptic paper as it tests all the skills you developed during AS (AO1, AO2 and AO3) but in a less compartmentalised way. Quality of written communication is assessed under AO3.

Timing

1 hour 30 minutes. Take care to reserve most of your time for the two essay questions.

Practicalities

Unlike the AS papers, there will be no ruled spaces under the questions for your answers. You will need to write in the general type of answer book used for most examinations in black ink. As this gives you no guidance on how much to write for particular questions, time yourself when you do practice papers to see what you can realistically achieve.
As well as the question paper there will be a Resource Booklet of documents.

2 *Using the documents*

You should be able to evaluate a wider range of more challenging, genuine source material than the brief documents specially written for the AS examination. The maximum length is likely to be 1,250 words. These provide background to an exercise in selecting choices of action according to certain criteria and then applying ethical theories and principles to an ethical dilemma. From the documents you need to select appropriate ideas, comments and information to support your reasoning and analysis.

The source material could take the form of:
- factual information in text form
- definitions
- opinion and argument
- numerical and statistical information
- visual presentations such as tables, diagrams, scattergraphs and pie charts
- statements from experts and interested parties, such as religious, environmental, social and political pressure groups

You need to identify and evaluate conflicting ideas and arguments within the source material, and explain how the ideas and arguments may be influenced by a range of factors. These could be the social, political, religious or moral views of the writers of the sources, so you should apply the credibility criteria covered in Unit 1, such as bias and vested interest, to discuss how seriously the sources should be taken in the decision-making process.

The evidence and reasoning in the documents also needs to be assessed in terms of its strengths and weaknesses, bearing in mind what you learnt in Units 1 and 2 about adequacy, relevance, problems with different types of evidence, such as statistics and data from surveys, flaws in reasoning, appeals to emotion and problems with hypothetical reasoning.

3 Short questions

There are likely to be several low-mark questions, for example:
- Identify several problems in defining one of the central concepts referred to in the documents. These could be controversial terms such as 'terrorism' or more abstract **moral concepts** such as 'duty'.
- Identify several problems in measuring the extent of one of the central concepts referred to in the documents, such as poverty.
- Identify and briefly explain a number of factors that might affect how people react to the issue.
- State and explain one **dilemma** that arises in making decisions about the key issue. Remember that a dilemma is a situation where a choice must be made between equally unfavourable, or mutually exclusive, options, which will each result in undesirable consequences as well as benefits. You may be able to identify a dilemma mentioned in the sources or need to construct a relevant one yourself, taking great care in how you express it.

4 Longer questions

4.1 Applying criteria to choices

- There is likely to be a question worth about 20 marks asking you to explain how the **choices** we could make about tackling the issue in the document are affected by **criteria** that are used in the **decision-making** process.
- The question paper may supply a number of choices and criteria for you to discuss, or you may be expected to work them out for yourself from the documents and your own experience.
- You need to demonstrate understanding of the idea that there may be a range of possible responses to complex moral and ethical problems, such as introducing new legislation, changes in administration, arousing public awareness or taking no action.
- Many different criteria could be applied in assessing the value and effectiveness of different solutions, e.g. public opinion, cost, practicality, social, political and environmental considerations.
- In the course of answering this question you should try to refer to most of the documents and succinctly assess the relevant views or information in them as you do so.
- Organise your response carefully. Subheadings relating to the different criteria or choices may help to guide the reader. Remember to write a conclusion.

4.2 Attempting to resolve a dilemma

The highest-mark question on the paper is likely to be worth about 30 marks, asking you to write an argument that attempts to resolve the dilemma you have identified.

- In your argument you should identify and apply relevant principles, which may be derived from ethical theories.
- Take two or preferably three **moral principles** or **ethical theories** (also known as **ethical positions**) in turn and discuss how supporters of these positions would be likely to view the dilemma.
- Your answer should be supported with material from the Resource Booklet using as many documents as are relevant (but do not repeat criticisms already made of the material).
- You are not expected to have detailed theoretical knowledge of ethical theories and principles and will not be rewarded for simply summarising them without making their relevance clear. However, you do need to be able to apply named ethical theories such as *some* of the following:
  - **Deontological theories or duty ethics**, referring to ideas such as Kant's categorical imperative and universalisability principle (means and ends), John Rawls' veil of ignorance, W. D. Ross' conflicting duties.
  - **Teleological or consequentialist theories** such as utilitarianism, referring to ideas such as Bentham's act utilitarianism and the hedonic calculus, John Stuart Mill's rule utilitarianism, Peter Singer's preference utilitarianism and prudentialism (also known as the precautionary principle).
  - **Libertarianism**, referring to ideas such as those of Robert Nozick and Milton Friedman and policies of the American Libertarian Party. In the UK libertarians oppose the 'nanny state'.
  - **Paternalism**, defending the vulnerable from harming themselves.
  - **Natural Law**, such as the ideas of Aristotle and Thomas Aquinas.
  - **Human rights and social contract**, striking a balance between people's responsibility to abide by the law and rights to civil liberties as explored by Thomas Hobbes, John Locke and Jean-Jacques Rousseau; long-established rights such as not being imprisoned without a definite charge being made (the Habeas Corpus Act of 1679); international human rights agreements and legislation such as the terms of the 1948 Universal Declaration of Human Rights, the European Convention of Human Rights and Human Rights Act 1998.
  - **Egalitarianism and left-wing theories** such as Marxism.
  - **Egoism**, prioritising one's own needs and ambitions, as expressed through the ideas of Friedrich Nietzsche.
  - **Elitism**, such as Conservative ideas on independent and grammar schools.
  - **Altruism**, prioritising the needs of others.
  - If you are confident in the application of social, political and religious principles you have encountered in your studies in other subject areas, such as sociology, politics, economics, business, literary study, religious studies and philosophy, you can apply them if they seem relevant, providing you remain objective.
  - Less-developed ethical principles such as 'We should treat people as equal' and 'Fairness is essential'.
- Your answer to this question needs to be a coherent essay examining alternatives in the form of argument, sustained counter-argument and suppositional reasoning.

- As you will be assessed for communication, you must use terminology appropriately and show understanding of a range of language relevant to moral and ethical problems such as: rights; needs; means, end, entitlement; deserts; values; deonto-logical, consequentialist, elitist and altruistic.
- You should apply hypothetical reasoning by assessing the likely consequences of alternative courses of action.
- Ensure that you do full justice to a range of possible views, resisting the temptation to oversimplify the issues. Finally, even though by its very nature, a dilemma can never be resolved to eliminate all problems, you should conclude by identifying the ethical theory or principle which suggests the most satisfactory resolution and explaining your choice.

UNIT 4 Critical reasoning

A Analysis

1 Familiar elements of arguments

Begin by revising the components or elements of argument from the specification for Units 1 and 2, with which you should already be familiar. Ensure that you know the standard notations (abbreviations) for components used in diagrams, though it is probably clearer to use the appropriate words when writing essays analysing the argument structure. You will notice that some of the elements of argument do not have widely accepted abbreviations. Do not be tempted to make up your own abbreviations for these, as several begin with the same letter and this could cause confusion. Use the earlier chapters of this book and any other textbooks or class notes you have to check over the definitions. You need to be able to recognise and write about the functions in a particular context of the following:

- argument
- claim or assertion
- main or overall conclusion (C)
- reason (R)
- evidence (Ev)
- example (Ex)
- intermediate conclusion (IC)
- counter-argument (CA)
- counter-claim or counter-assertion (CC)
- response or challenge to counter-argument (RCA)
- response or challenge to counter-claim (RCC)
- counter-example
- assumption (A)
- principle (P)
- hypothetical or suppositional reasoning (HR)
- analogy (Ag)

1.1 Counter-assertion, counter-claim or counter-argument?

Some of the textbooks you encounter may treat counter-assertions, counter-claims and counter-arguments as if they are the same thing, using the abbreviation CA for all. Similarly, they may blur the distinction between response to counter-argument and response to counter-assertion or response to counter-claim. The intention is probably to simplify matters for AS students, but by A2 you should be able to grasp the difference. 'Assertion' and 'claim' are different words for the same element, but 'argument' has a different meaning, and the same applies to the words associated with these terms. It is easy to compare them as follows:

- An assertion or claim draws a conclusion without giving reasons.
- An argument consists of conclusion plus reason(s).
- A counter-assertion or counter-claim opposes an argument without giving reasons.
- A counter-argument opposes an argument, giving reasons.

An example of a counter-assertion or counter-claim plus response is as follows:

> Some people think that flying to holiday destinations is acceptable (CC), but the public should try to find alternative means of transport (RCC).

An example of a counter-argument plus response is as follows:

> Some people think that flying to holiday destinations is acceptable, because the planes are going there anyway (CA) but the public should realise that by choosing alternative means of transport and thereby reducing demand they could help to protect the environment (RCA).

You should be able to see that the counter-argument consists of two parts:

> Some people think that flying to holiday destinations is acceptable (conclusion), because the planes are going there anyway (reason).

Because the reason for the opposing statement is provided, there is more for the challenger to argue with, so the response tends to be more substantial and in this case incorporates a short reason ('thereby reducing demand').

To avoid the possibility that CA may be taken for counter-assertion when you intend it to signify counter-argument, you may prefer to avoid the terms relating to assertions, substituting the words claim (for which there is no widely accepted abbreviation), counter-claim (CC) and response to counter-claim (RCC).

2 *Less familiar elements of arguments*

2.1 Scene setting

This refers to background material that often precedes an argument. A newspaper article may begin by providing some basic facts about an event or social trend and then, in the form of an argument, express views about what action should be taken. You may be required to distinguish the argument from the scene setting and explanation. Here is an example:

> The cleric described as Osama bin Laden's helper was released on bail yesterday, despite the Prime Minister's vows to protect the public against terror. Clearly there needs to be a change in the law that currently makes it impossible for us to deport dangerous people who may not receive a fair trial in their own countries. Few countries have such a fair legal system as ours, so this reasoning means we could be stuck with countless foreign offenders. This excessive concern for the underdog presents an unnecessary risk to our own population.

You should be able to see that the first sentence is scene setting and the argument that constitutes the rest of the passage is structurally complete without it. The scene setting suggests a reason for the arguer's current interest in the issue of foreign offenders' rights and the reference to this particular case is likely to make the reader more interested. Nevertheless the argument itself is more general, as its conclusion in the second sentence of the passage indicates.

2.2 Rhetorical devices

These are means of gaining and keeping the interest of the audience or reader. They are rarely part of the reasoning itself, but add to the emotional impact of the argument.

Consider this extract from a speech by Barack Obama when campaigning for President. It is very persuasive, yet it contains little that could be described as reasons or evidence. Most of it is rhetoric.

> Years from now, you'll look back and you'll say that this was the moment, this was the place where America remembered what it means to hope. For many months we've been teased, even derided, for talking about hope. But we always knew hope is not blind optimism. It's not ignoring the enormity of the task ahead or the roadblocks that stand in our path. It's not sitting on the sidelines or shirking from a fight. Hope is that thing inside us that insists, despite all the evidence to the contrary, that something better awaits us if we have the courage to reach for it, and to work for it, and to fight for it.

After reading the list of rhetorical devices and examples below, look back at the Obama speech and see which you can recognise. It is unnecessary for you to remember the names of all these devices, but they are provided for your interest.

Rhetorical question

This is a question intended for dramatic effect, not to draw an answer. An example is 'Who would be so mean as to refuse to help these poor people?'

Question asked by the speaker and then immediately answered

This device is known as **rogatio**. Martin Luther King used it in his famous 'I have a dream' speech in 1963: 'There are those who are asking the devotees of civil rights, "When will you be satisfied?" We can never be satisfied as long as the Negro is the victim of the unspeakable horrors of police brutality.'

A string of questions uttered in rapid succession for emotional emphasis

Greek orators called this **quaestitio**. In Shakespeare's *The Merchant of Venice*, a speech by the Jewish money lender Shylock makes use of this technique:

> Hath not a Jew eyes? hath not a Jew hands, organs,
> dimensions, senses, affections, passions? fed with
> the same food, hurt with the same weapons, subject
> to the same diseases, healed by the same means,
> warmed and cooled by the same winter and summer, as
> a Christian is?

Repetition

Martin Luther King made substantial use of this device:

> Let freedom ring from Lookout Mountain of Tennessee! Let freedom ring from every hill and molehill of Mississippi. From every mountainside, let freedom ring.

Parallelism

Several parts of a sentence or several sentences are similarly structured to draw attention to the links between the ideas through the rhythm. Hillary Clinton used this device in her campaign for the American presidency in 2008:

> We're going on, we're going strong and we're going all the way!

Antithesis

This means establishing an obvious contrast between ideas by juxtaposing them, often in a parallel structure. Hillary Clinton used the device to describe what she hoped was an improved chance of being elected as presidential candidate after several setbacks:

For everybody who has ever been counted out and refused to be knocked out, for everyone who has stumbled and stood right back up and for everybody who works hard and never gives up — this one's for you.

Tricolon

This device involves making a three-part statement, using similar syntax. Both of Hillary Clinton's speeches above make use of the three-part structure.

A four-part statement is known as a tetracolon but these are rarer, perhaps reflecting the limited attention span of the average audience. Martin Luther King was a compelling enough speaker to get away with it. Note also the antithesis between the first sentence and the next four:

> This is no time to engage in the luxury of cooling off or to take the tranquilizing drug of gradualism. Now is the time to make real the promises of democracy. Now is the time to rise from the dark and desolate valley of segregation to the sunlit path of racial justice. Now is the time to lift our nation from the quick sands of racial injustice to the solid rock of brotherhood. Now is the time to make justice a reality for all of God's children.

Hyperbole

This is the use of excessive, often exaggerated language designed to stir the audience or reader, for example when Martin Luther King said:

> I have a dream that one day even the state of Mississippi, a state sweltering with the heat of injustice, sweltering with the heat of oppression, will be transformed into an oasis of freedom and justice.

Expletive

This is a short phrase interrupting the syntax of the sentence. It is often put in for extra emphasis or persuasion, for example the phrases 'believe me', 'of course', 'friends' and 'fellow Americans'.

2.3 Appeals

Appeals to emotions such as fear, hatred or sympathy are a type of rhetorical device. They are intended to play the role of reasons or evidence in arguments by persuading the reader to accept the conclusion. A charity encouraging the public to sponsor children in developing countries includes in its publicity material the rhetorical question 'Imagine changing the life of a child like Elsy?', accompanied by an attractive photograph. Appeals may help to carry the argument by influencing the reader's emotions rather than by providing logical reasons to support the conclusion. These will be examined more fully in the section on evaluation below.

2.4 Rant

Rant is an emotional assertion of opinion. It may be supported by no reasons at all or by reasons or evidence which lack any real substance and simply provides a rhetorical flourish. Rant may appear on the surface to be argument but it is not.

2.5 Strands of reasoning

This refers to the various groups of arguments and counter-arguments that constitute a longer argument or article. In the long passages you analyse at A2, the writer is likely

to pursue various lines of thought in different paragraphs, often providing several reasons and pieces of evidence to support an intermediate conclusion. One strand of reasoning might support an intermediate conclusion by extended analogy and another by developed hypothetical reasoning.

2.6 Move

A move is a switch from one strand of reasoning to another, implying that there is some connection between them. For example, the writer might reveal a UK problem in one strand of reasoning and argue for immediate action and then move to describing the way a supposedly similar problem has been dealt with abroad. You might be asked to evaluate how effective this move is.

2.7 Independent and joint reasons and chains of reasoning

A conclusion may be supported by one reason or several. Independent or side-by-side reasons may make the argument more persuasive by their accumulative effect, but the conclusion could still be reached if supported by only one of them. Here is an example:

> You should visit the Tutankhamun exhibition in London because the treasures on display are said to be the most spectacular archaeological finds anywhere in the world and you will need something interesting to do in the school holidays.

In this case you could imagine the arguer adding more independent reasons, such as special price offers, the fact that everyone will be talking about it and so on, to induce the listener to visit the exhibition.

In contrast joint reasons work together to support the conclusion, as in the following example:

> You should visit the Tutankhamun exhibition in London because the treasures are not going to be on display in any other European city and you are unlikely to be able to afford to visit them when they return to Egypt.

Here if either of the reasons was absent, the conclusion would not be reached. It is only the combination of the unavailability of the treasures in Europe and the prohibitive cost of seeing them in Egypt that makes the argument persuasive. Joint reasons work together as a series of steps, and three or more reasons working in this way are known as a chain of reasoning.

2.8 Sustained suppositional reasoning

At AS, candidates may be asked to identify an example of hypothetical reasoning. These usually follow the 'if A, then B structure' and tend to be confined to a single sentence. In A2 passages you may be more likely to encounter sustained suppositional reasoning embedded in a strand of argument, but you will be expected to identify it for yourself and perhaps comment on its effectiveness as part of a general evaluation.

Suppositional argument means exploring one or more suppositions or imaginary scenarios in order to think more clearly about a situation and perhaps solve a problem or decide upon a course of action. Nigel Warburton provides a good example of a brief piece of suppositional reasoning in his excellent book *Thinking from A to Z* (1996):

Supposition: A premise assumed for the sake of argument but not necessarily believed: sometimes known as a presupposition. Suppositions, unlike assertions, are not presumed to be true: rather they are instrumental in finding out what is true.

For example, a police inspector might say the following, 'Let's suppose the murderer did enter the house by the window. Surely we'd expect to find some evidence of forced entry.' The inspector is not asserting that the murderer definitely did enter the house; nor even that that is probably what happened. The inspector is inviting us to follow through a chain of reasoning based on the supposition that the murderer came in through the window. In other words the inspector is offering a hypothesis about what might have happened.

If Warburton had provided the complete chain of reasoning, revealing whether there was evidence of forced entry and what it might mean, this could have been developed into sustained suppositional reasoning.

3 *Practising skills of analysis*

Try to answer these questions on the following article by Janet Street-Porter, which is organised in such a way as to make the task quite challenging.

A return to the ration book is the answer to obesity

1 A whopping number of kids — around a quarter — are now officially overweight before they've even started primary school, according to new statistics released by the Department of Health. It has only taken a couple of generations for small children to morph from skinny live wires into chubby couch potatoes who sit glued to their screens, don't walk anywhere and who shun the idea of sporting activity.

2 When I look back at pictures of me as a child, I look skeletal by today's standards — in 2008 any mum with small children the size we were back in the 1950s would be hauled before a child protection agency and accused of starving her offspring.

3 The fact is, my parents went through rationing during and after the war, and were thinner because they ate much less meat and protein, exercised more and, even, though money was short, ate more fresh food and far less processed muck.

4 Now we've got more money and allegedly a higher standard of living, but no sense of when to stop eating. And don't tell me it's about poverty — if a third of the nation's 11-year olds are overweight before they start secondary school, it's a disease that affects all classes and income levels.

5 The government is waffling about inspecting lunch boxes — an idea that will never work. What we need is dead simple. Bring back rationing. Don't talk to me about human rights — at this rate one third of the younger generation aren't going to make it past 50 before they peg out from heart failure.

6 Evil fatty processed foods should be strictly rationed with government stamps and ration books. We should be limited to strict quotas of meat per person per week, allowed unlimited fresh fruit and vegetables. Sugar, chocolate, fats salt should only be available with coupons. Yes, it's drastic — but look where free choice has got us.

(*Independent on Sunday*, 24 February 2008)

A *Analysis*

1 Identify and briefly explain the function of the following elements in the structure of Street-Porter's argument.

   (a) 'in 2008 any mum with small children the size we were back in the 1950s would be hauled before a child protection agency and accused of starving her offspring' (paragraph 2)   *(2 marks)*

   (b) 'The fact is, my parents went through rationing during and after the war, and were thinner because they ate much less meat and protein, exercised more and, even, though money was short, ate more fresh food and far less processed muck' (paragraph 3)

(2 marks)

   (c) 'Evil fatty processed foods should be strictly rationed with government stamps and ration books' (paragraph 6)   *(2 marks)*

   (d) 'Yes, it's drastic' (paragraph 6)   *(2 marks)*

   (e) 'but look where free choice has got us' (paragraph 6)   *(2 marks)*

2 Analyse in detail the structure of the reasoning in paragraphs 4 and 5.

(12 marks)

Notice that there are 2 marks for each of the shorter questions so try to answer with more than a couple of words. Naming the component correctly will probably gain you one mark, but it is advisable also to relate it briefly to other parts of the argument to establish clearly what its function is, as follows:

1   **(a)** Hypothetical argument, used by Street-Porter to support her earlier observation that small children have morphed from skinny to chubby in 'a couple of generations'.

   (b) This is an analogy. It serves as a reason for the conclusion 'Bring back rationing' by showing that in the past rationing made people thinner, so by implication the same could happen again.

   (c) This with the following two sentences serve as an amplification of the conclusion 'Bring back rationing', providing more detail as to how it should be done. The argument is structurally complete without it but it acts as a sort of footnote.

   (d) This is a counter-claim to the detailed suggestions of rationing, already anticipated by the word 'yes'.

   (e) 'but look where free choice has got us' is a response to the counter-claim that precedes it. It is rhetorical, referring back implicitly to paragraph 4's statement that we have no sense when to stop eating.

2   Paragraph 4 continues the strand of argument from the previous three paragraphs establishing the contrast between the body size and circumstances of people nowadays and two generations ago. The first sentence provides a reason for the current problem identified at the very beginning of the argument 'Now we've got…no sense when to stop eating'. This is followed by a challenge to an anticipated counter-argument in which an imagined opponent suggests obesity is just a problem for the poor because they can only afford fattening foods.

The author challenges this with a response to the counterargument ('And don't tell me it's about poverty') followed by a reason for the challenge; if a third of 11 year olds are overweight this is a disease affecting all income levels.

Paragraph 5 begins with what is an alternative to her own conclusion, the lunchbox inspection suggestion, which therefore acts as a counter-claim, one that is rapidly dismissed as 'an idea that will never work' (response to the counter-claim). 'What we need is dead simple' is an intermediate conclusion, leading on to the conclusion of the whole argument 'Bring back rationing'. The paragraph ends with a challenge to another anticipated counter-argument (that rationing should not be allowed because it is contrary to human rights). The response to the counter-argument is 'Don't talk to me about human rights' and this is supported by a reason, implying that human rights are not the greatest priority and predicting that 'At this rate one third of the younger generation aren't going to make it past 50'.

Answers to question 2 will be assigned to levels, as in the case of the longer questions in other units. The criteria for Level 4, the highest level, worth 10–12 marks, are as follows:

Criteria for top-level marks
- Candidates demonstrate thorough understanding of argument structure.
- They are able to identify elements of complex reasoning accurately, using appropriate terminology.
- Mistakes are rare and not serious.

As you may find analysing real media articles quite challenging, it may encourage you to know that candidates 'may make mistakes, occasionally serious ones' and still be awarded Level 3 (7–9 marks) providing most of the elements of reasoning are identified accurately. You are advised to read the key paragraphs more than once before writing down your analysis as you may change your mind after closer scrutiny.

If you wish you can write out phrases or sentences from the passage in the form of a list and indicate what components they are using standard abbreviations such as R1, Ev and IC. Alternatively a verbal account such as the one above could be accompanied by a diagram clarifying the structure of the argument. Some verbal explanation is always going to be necessary as there may be some components, such as scene setting, for which there are not well-established abbreviations. In addition real arguments tend to have subtleties and complexities which are more easily conveyed in words.

B Evaluation

Begin by reminding yourself of the strengths and weaknesses in reasoning and evidence first met in Units 1 and 2, including the definitions of specific flaws. Any of these could be encountered again in Unit 4 but they will not be flagged up for your attention in such an obvious way as before. Make sure that you could recognise them in context and explain why such types of reasoning can strengthen or weaken an argument.

1 Familiar strengths in arguments and evidence

Familiar strengths include the following:
- reputation of author or sources high
- ability to see, eyewitness account
- no known vested interest
- expertise in relevant field
- neutrality, unbiased, balanced account exploring opposing viewpoints
- consistency
- reasonableness and plausibility
- evidence relevant, up to date and detailed
- research well conducted, based on large representative samples
- statistics and examples convincing

2 Familiar weaknesses and flaws in arguments

Familiar weaknesses and flaws include:
- reasons that are inadequate so conclusions are overdrawn
- irrelevance
- ambiguity of terms
- slippery slope
- post hoc
- circular argument (begging the question)
- restricting the options (false dichotomy)
- conflation
- confusing cause and effect, correlation equals cause confusion and other errors relating to causation
- *tu quoque* or reasoning from wrong actions
- confusing necessary and sufficient conditions
- hasty or unwarranted or sweeping generalisation
- straw person or straw man
- *ad hominem*
- arguing from one thing to another
- problems with evidence such misleading statistics or small, unrepresentative samples
- false assumptions
- disanalogies (poor analogies)
- failure to meet credibility criteria (CRAVEN)

3 Evaluating assumptions

A more sophisticated approach to assumptions will be expected than at AS. As well as identifying their presence when analysing the structure of arguments, you may need to identify and assess them when evaluating the quality of reasoning in a strand of argument. This is likely to involve:
- judging whether or not they are reasonable assumptions

- stating whether what is assumed is a fact that can easily be established, one that would be difficult to investigate or an opinion or principle that people might disagree about
- evaluating the extent to which the strand of argument and perhaps the whole argument is weakened if the assumption is not justified

4 *Evaluating analogies*

You should recall from AS that an analogy is a comparison often used for purposes of persuasion. At A2 you will be expected to notice analogies embedded in a passage for yourself, rather than being directed towards them. You will need to:

- recognise the situations that are being compared
- identify any mistaken facts or generalisations made about either of the items being compared
- assess the analogy for relevant similarities and differences
- evaluate whether the analogy is an apt one
- show awareness of whether the analogy is sustained and is crucial to the argument or is simply an add-on extra
- assess the impact of the use of analogy on the strength or weakness of the reasoning in that strand of the argument or the whole argument

5 *Evaluating sustained suppositional reasoning*

Here is an example of suppositional reasoning that is more sustained than the one earlier about the murder:

> Should taking cannabis be legalised, should the penalties be harsher or should they remain the same? Let us explore the possibilities.
>
> Suppose cannabis taking were legalised. This would save police and court time as they would no longer have to prosecute those whose only offence was being found in possession of the drug. Drugs sold in ordinary shops could have their contents regulated, making it impossible for drug pushers to contaminate cannabis with more dangerous and expensive drugs in the hope of getting customers hooked. On the other hand, unless there were no age restrictions, there would be a need to punish attempts to sell the drugs to children so this would still take up police time. Cannabis is known to cause both mental and physical illness in some consumers, and the personal and economic costs of this would need to be taken into account.
>
> Supposing instead we increased the penalties for taking the drug. This might discourage some people, safeguarding their health but it would be detrimental to those suffering from certain conditions, such as multiple sclerosis, which are said to be relieved by the drug…

After following through the implications of all three positions, the above argument would conclude by recommending the position likely to have the best outcome.

How would you assess such an argument? The reasoning, except for the consideration of the current position, is all based on hypothesis about what could happen, so can neither be refuted nor proved correct. However, your task would be to scrutinise the suggestions made and decide whether they are reasonable, biased or selective.

Are there other important possibilities which are omitted, ones that could have changed the balance and resulted in a different conclusion? Are all the premises and assumptions

reasonable? For example, is it likely that people would be able to buy cannabis from 'ordinary shops' or is it more probable that there would be some sort of regulation, for example through doctors' prescriptions, to prevent harm to those under age or mentally ill? Would punishment of those selling to the under-age necessarily be police business or could it be handled by some health or trading standards agency? Could those suffering from multiple sclerosis be excluded from harsher penalties imposed on cannabis takers, making this counter-example less significant?

The reasoning required for this task is little different from the way you would evaluate other types of argument.

6   *Deductive reasoning*

The study of valid and invalid forms of argument is a new element of Unit 4. Most of the arguments you will have encountered so far are **inductive** arguments. These are ones where reasoning leads us to suppose there is a high probability that the claim is true, but there could always be a slight element of doubt. Scientific theories are often based on the results of experiments repeated a reasonable number of times. Similarly conclusions in the social sciences arise from studies of a sample of people considered to be sufficiently large and representative. Induction is therefore based on an accumulation of evidence, leading to a conclusion that is highly **probable**. However, it would be wrong to describe these conclusions as 'proved'.

In contrast **deductive reasoning** involves a logical working out of a conclusion, rather like in mathematics. The conclusions are **certainly** true if the reasons are true and the structure of the argument is **valid**.

6.1 Valid deductions

There are two valid forms of **hypothetical argument** which are quite easy to recognise. They are usually expressed in the form of two sentences, each of which has two parts. The first sentence (the **premise**) has the familiar 'if A then B' structure:

> If Jon gets three grade As at A-level, he will be accepted by Oxford University.

The first part of this sentence is called the antecedent and the second part the consequent.

The second sentence draws the conclusion:

> Jon has obtained three grade As now so he will be accepted by Oxford University.

This form of argument is known as **affirming the antecedent**, because conditions set in the first part of the first sentence have been achieved. Providing the first statement is true, the second must logically follow. This valid structure is also known as **modus ponens**.

Denying the consequent, also known as **modus tollens**, is another valid structure:

> If Jon gets three grade As at A-level, he will be accepted by Oxford University.
>
> I have just heard that Jon was not accepted by Oxford so he can't have got his three As.

In this case it is the consequent that has not been achieved, so we can deduce the required conditions were not met.

6.2 Formal fallacies

Unfortunately there are two patterns of argument that look similar to those above but which are not valid. The premises can be true without the conclusions being true. They are known as formal fallacies because their form is misleading. They are as follows:

Affirming the consequent

> If Jon gets three grade As at A-level, he will be accepted by Oxford University.
>
> Jon has been accepted by Oxford so he must have got his three As.

This is not necessarily true. The premise was not that Jon would only be accepted if he got three As. Sometimes universities accept students who just fail to meet their conditions, especially if they impress in some other way, such as taking critical thinking as a fourth A-level!

Denying the antecedent

> If Jon gets three grade As at A-level, he will be accepted by Oxford University.
>
> Jon has not managed to get three As so he won't be accepted by Oxford University.

In this structure the second sentence begins with a negative form of the antecedent of the first sentence. The conclusion may turn out to be true but it is not certain, for the same reason given above. The admissions tutor may be generous.

6.3 Syllogisms

There is another form of logical argument called a **syllogism**. It is a deductive argument with two premises followed by a conclusion. Each part contains a different combination of two of the three terms mentioned in the argument. A valid form of the syllogism has the following simple structure:

> All As are B.
>
> C is A.
>
> Therefore C is B.

Its structure guarantees that the conclusion must be true if both premises are true. A simple example is as follows:

> All mammals are warm-blooded.
>
> Rats are mammals.
>
> Therefore rats must have warm blood.

In an everyday context you are more likely to see an informal version of this type of argument, as in this example:

> The Chinese restaurant has a deal where you can eat as much as you want for £10 on Mondays. Jake has an enormous appetite so you should take him to the restaurant on a Monday.

You could rewrite it unkindly as follows:

Greedy people (A) visit the restaurant on Mondays (B).

Jake (C) is a greedy person (A).

Therefore Jake (C) should go on a Monday (B).

People are sometimes misled by an argument that closely resembles this form, known as the **fallacy of the undistributed middle**.

All mammals are warm-blooded.

Birds are warm-blooded.

So birds must be mammals.

The difference begins in the form of the second premise. The argument runs as follows:

All As are B.

C is B.

Therefore C is A.

This fallacy gets its name from the term that occurs in both premises, in this case warm-bloodedness. It is undistributed because its use does not apply exclusively either to mammals or to birds, so it cannot be used to argue that birds and mammals are the same.

It is easy to see how people can make the undistributed middle error. Here is another example of it:

Students (A) get concessions at the cinema (B).

That old lady (C) has just obtained a cheap ticket (B).

She (C) must be a student (A).

While this could be so, it is more likely that the old lady got a pensioner's concession. Concessions at the cinema are not confined to students; they apply to retired people and cinema staff as well.

You may notice that this structure closely resembles the examples above of the deductively invalid form affirming the consequent.

The rules concerning syllogisms and similar-looking arguments occupy many pages of books on logic, often explained by diagrams. Unless you particularly enjoy studying these, the best advice is simply to be alert for key words and structures such as 'if…so' and 'all…therefore'. If you are faced with a confusing argument that appears to have a similar structure to the syllogism, it can be helpful to mentally change some of the parts to examples you find easy to think about. Always bear in mind that the initial premise may be false or a sweeping generalisation, in which case the conclusion may be unsound, regardless of the precise form of the argument.

6.4 False converse

Changing round the key terms of a two-part statement produces its **converse**. People sometimes think that the converse of a true conditional proposition will also be true, but this is often not the case. Assume that the true statement is as follows:

If it is raining, then the school fete will be cancelled.

Now consider the converse:

If the school fete is cancelled, then it will be raining.

This is not necessarily the case, as the fete might be cancelled for other reasons, such as lack of support.

6.5 Law of excluded middle versus fuzzy logic

Having looked briefly at logic, we ought to bear in mind its limitations too. According to classical logic, propositions obey the **law of excluded middle**, which states that every proposition must be either true or false. Any middle position between truth and falsity is excluded. It follows that, for any given statement and the negation of that statement, if one is true, the other must be false.

More recently philosophers have become interested in **subjectivity**, the notion that propositions might be possible but uncertain and that there could be degrees of truth. This is known as **fuzzy logic**. It is an oversimplification to think in terms of binary oppositions, dividing statements into those that are definitely true and those that are definitely untrue. This idea is also known as the 'black or white fallacy'. You can see its relevance if you consider the statements: *Tony Blair was a good Prime Minister* and *Tony Blair was not a good Prime Minister*. Many people would tend to agree to some extent with both statements for different reasons.

7 *Evaluating appeals*

Revise the appeals you learnt in the AS course: appeals to popularity, history and such emotions as pity, fear and hatred. These are often regarded as weaknesses in argument as they employ loaded words such as 'terrorists', 'victim' and 'brutality' to arouse the feelings of the reader rather than providing sound evidence. However, emotional appeals can contribute to the force of an argument if used together with logical reasoning and compelling evidence. An appeal to fear can be valid if it is accompanied by truthful evidence of what may happen if precautions are not taken.

'Beware! Touching this hotplate could cause serious burns' does arouse emotions in the reader but they serve to reinforce an important message, the truth of which could easily be tested.

In contrast Enoch Powell's famous 'rivers of blood' speech about curbing immigration to Britain contained many appeals to fear that were not backed by sound reasoning and evidence. For example, the prediction that Powell quoted from a member of the public, 'In this country in 15 or 20 years' time the black man will have the whip hand over the white man', had the capacity to arouse fear and hatred without providing any evidence to support it. The phrase 'whip hand' was particularly emotive, as it conjured up the image of blacks enslaving whites. The fact that the prediction was made in 1968 about a Britain two decades into the future makes it demonstrably clear that this was a misleading appeal to emotion.

Below is a more thorough list of appeals than you are likely to have encountered before. These are not included in the list of appeals on the OCR specification, so do not feel that you have to learn them all, but you may begin to recognise many of them in the documents you encounter. The Latin names are provided in case you happen to be interested, but you could identify them by the English names or your own apt description and explain their effects in particular contexts.

- *ad baculum*: this involves threatening opponents with force or the imposition of an unpleasant penalty if they do not agree with the conclusion; also look out for its opposite, an appeal to bribery, offering some sort of inducement to those who agree to the argument
- *ad crumenam*, relating to money; this involves an argument that because someone is paid well, they must do a good job, or if a product is expensive it must be of good quality; 'You get what you pay for' is sometimes untrue
- *ad invidium*, appeal to envy; this is used a great deal by advertisers
- *ad lazarum*, appeal to poverty; this suggests that the poor and humble are more in touch with reality so their view is likely to be true
- *ad nauseam*, repeating the same point over and over again so that the opponent sickens and gives in
- *ad novitam*, appeal to novelty; advertisers make much use of our readiness to be impressed by something new and modern
- *ad populum*, appealing to popular prejudices, regardless of whether they are based on truth; British National Party propaganda uses such techniques, for example citing the view that the country is being overrun by asylum seekers
- *ad superstitionem*, appeal to superstition
- *ad superbium*, appeal to pride
- *ad temperantium*, appealing to people's feelings that a moderate position or compromise must be a better choice than one that is made to appear extreme or radical
- *sentimens superior*, suggesting that feelings are a better guide than reason

7.1 Appeal to authority

This is not an emotional appeal like those above. A writer or speaker may quote from the Bible or the Koran or refer to a well-known saying or precedent to add weight to their argument. Using statistics or specialist terms may also add to the impression of expertise, increasing credibility. Although appeals to inappropriate or unnamed authorities tended to be viewed as weaknesses in reasoning in Unit 2, an appeal to a relevant authority, especially where there is no evidence of disagreement from other authority figures, may strengthen an argument.

You can read more about appeals on the following website: **www.skeptics.org.uk/ forum/showthread.php?t=446**

8 *Putting your evaluation skills into practice*

Let us turn again to the Janet Street-Porter article (page 106) that we analysed earlier and attempt some evaluation questions.

> Street-Porter's article claims in its title that 'a return to the ration book is the answer to obesity'. Evaluate the support given to this claim by her reasoning

in paragraphs 1 to 5. You should consider how specific strengths and weaknesses in the reasoning impact upon the support given to this claim.

(10 marks)

This question is quite challenging because the passage has not been deliberately written to contain flaws, unlike those in Units 1 and 2. In fact the article provided in this unit, usually by a well-known writer, is likely to have been considered sufficiently convincing to be published in the national press. Thus it may take you longer to identify any weaknesses and they may be fairly subtle, although some should fall into familiar categories such as assumption, slippery slope, generalisation, inconsistency and so on. Here are some tips:

- Try to make a variety of points, for example by referring to single examples of different named flaws as opposed to multiple examples of the same flaw. This will demonstrate broader knowledge to the examiner.
- Think of a precise way to describe the argument's strengths, which we tend to take for granted. The CRAVEN criteria learnt in Unit 1 may be helpful.
- Remember to consider rhetorical devices such as appeals, which can be seen as flaws if they are not backed by reasoned argument and convincing evidence.
- Read through the passage carefully and underline in pencil any points that strike you as possible strengths or weaknesses. In the case of weaknesses, decide which are important enough to affect the overall credibility and persuasiveness of the article and write about these rather than minor quibbles.
- As well as examining the precise content of the article, give some thought to any important issues which should have been considered but have been neglected, as this will enable you to reach a holistic judgement about the effectiveness of the argument.
- Before you begin to write, organise your points logically, for example by grouping the strengths and weaknesses or by working chronologically through the article.
- It is not expected that you will discuss every possible strength and weakness in the article and indeed some questions specifically remind you to be 'selective'. This is another occasion where you should calculate how much time you should spend on this particular question, considering the marks allocated in relation to the total marks for the paper and the length of the examination. (Based on the OCR specimen paper this would be 15 minutes.) By attempting several similar tasks and timing yourself, try to form an idea of how much well-considered material you can write in this time. This should help in your planning and selection of material.
- Do not be tempted to continue writing after the time you have allocated to the question has elapsed. This will be counterproductive by diminishing the attention you can give to later questions, while not necessarily increasing the marks you earn for this one.

Here is a suggested response covering many of the points that could be made, though it is unlikely that many candidates would be able to write so much in the time limit:

> Street-Porter's article makes use of emotional appeals, but nevertheless she sometimes backs up her points with convincing evidence. 'Whopping' is a loaded word, designed to shock the reader. However, the author justifies its use by the statistics she provides which, although somewhat vague ('around a quarter') sound credible because they come from an expert source, the Department of Health.

Street-Porter's second claim, that children 'sit glued to their screens, don't walk anywhere and (who) shun the idea of sporting activity' is less convincing as it is not supported by evidence. It is a sweeping generalisation perhaps based on stereotypes of the young. Worse than this, it may undermine her later conclusion. If children really are so inactive, it may be more logical to address their lack of exercise than to ration their food.

The evidence in the second and third paragraphs is based on personal experience rather than objective research. The list of factors affecting the author's parents makes it difficult for the reader to separate what appear to be the benefits of rationing to those of exercise. Street-Porter relies too much for her credibility on readers' own knowledge of war conditions; those who have heard of spam but know little else may have reason to doubt that 'there was far less processed muck'.

In the fourth paragraph her hasty generalisation that we have 'no sense of when to stop eating' is unsupported by evidence, and adds to the confusion of the argument. Street-Porter is conflating eating too much with eating the wrong type of food and probably intended to write the latter. In her final paragraph she recommends rationing unhealthy foods but allowing unlimited fresh fruit and vegetables, suggesting it is the nature of people's diets rather than how much they eat that concerns her. Nevertheless under her proposed scheme people with 'no sense of when to stop eating' could still become obese on unlimited potatoes and bananas.

Street-Porter makes an assumption that somewhat weakens her argument. She assumes that because as many as a third of 11 year olds are overweight, this must affect 'all incomes and classes', but this is not necessarily the case. If the problem is concentrated in the bottom third of the population with respect to income, then an alternative solution to the one proposed could be to subsidise healthier food and tax 'evil' processed foods, accompanied by a health education campaign.

The claim that the third of 11 year olds that are now overweight will die of heart failure by 50 is a prediction not backed by evidence. It appeals to the reader's fear but takes no account of the possibility that some children may become more health-conscious as they mature. The projection into the future does not allow for the possibility that anti-obesity campaigns may be effective without the need for rationing.

To conclude, Street-Porter initially makes quite a strong case concerning the need for action by citing the Department of Health, but she is imprecise about whether the cause of the problem is eating too much, eating the wrong food or lack of exercise, providing little expert evidence. If all three, it is unlikely that her proposed rationing scheme would solve the problem, although it might reduce it. She also gives no consideration as to how the public could be persuaded to accept a measure that she herself admits is 'drastic'.

The OCR descriptor of the standard of work expected of candidates placed in the top band for this type of question (worth 7–10 marks) is as follows:

Note the second point, which makes it clear that you are not expected to write everything there is to say on the matter, although the word 'thorough' in the previous point indicates that you should work quickly and accomplish as much as you possibly can.

The final point suggests that, after examining specific strengths and weaknesses, an overview is needed, hence the inclusion of the final paragraph in the specimen answer above. Remember that a holistic view of the argument is required in this unit, as opposed to the fragmented approach in Units 1 and 2 where there are lots of questions about the flaws and strengths in particular paragraphs.

8.1 Evaluating moves

Sometimes questions invite you to evaluate an author's **move** from one part of the argument to the other. The article by Street-Porter is shorter than a typical examination piece so the number of moves is limited. However, you should still be able to identify that there is a move from observing that children in the past used to be thinner to predicting that the current generation of children are in danger of dying by 50. This is followed by the move proposing rationing. Evaluating moves means discussing whether they follow logically and convincingly from each other. If you reread the more general evaluation of the passage above, you should be able to pick out some relevant comments. These could be rephrased and embellished to meet the needs of a specific question evaluating a move. The first one could be assessed as follows:

> Street-Porter's move from observing that children in the past used to be thinner to her prediction that 'one third of the younger generation aren't going to make it past 50' is problematical as the reasoning is flawed in two respects.
>
> She takes it for granted that being 'officially overweight' is less healthy than being 'skeletal'. Despite mentioning the Department of Health she supplies no scientific evidence of the dangers of being 'officially overweight'. Though it could be assumed that readers will already be convinced by this, it is obesity that is most frequently associated with high risk. Of the 'third of the nation's 11-year olds [who] are overweight', a much smaller proportion will be obese and some will only be marginally overweight.
>
> Furthermore her projection into the future does not allow for the possibility that anti-obesity campaigns may be effective in persuading today's 11 year olds to adopt healthier lifestyles as they mature.

Requirements for top-level marks in this type of question are very similar to those listed above. A selection of points about specific strengths or weaknesses in the author's reasoning in her move from one claim to the next is required. In addition there should be an overall assessment of how convincing and logical the move is. In the example above, this assessment comes first.

8.2 Evaluating a linked passage

Another type of question provides a second short passage in which a different author has either responded to the first article or independently expressed an alternative view. You could be asked to evaluate the second argument as it stands or to assess how effectively it counters the first. Here is the response of a blogger to the Street-Porter article:

> Do you really want to cut childhood obesity? Start a war. This will ensure that more women stay at home to look after the kids and cook them proper food. People will respect their elders. And supply routes for food will be cut.
>
> (Independent on Sunday message board, 2 March 2008, findarticles.com)

How would you describe this type of response? You might describe it as a straw person, as the blogger has picked up Street-Porter's reference to one apparently beneficial aspect of war, rationing, and expanded upon it to suggest, tongue in cheek, that we should start a war to achieve conditions that would reduce people's weight.

Alternatively, it could be described as a **reductio ad absurdum** as a ridiculous outcome is derived by appearing to accept Street-Porter's suggestions that lifestyles were better in wartime.

The blogger's response is really rant. It is weak on two counts. First, there is no reasoned argument seriously addressing any of the issues raised by Street-Porter or suggesting alternative solutions. Second, what Street-Porter has said is distorted, as she does not explicitly blame obesity on lack of home cooking and makes no reference at all to lack of respect for elders, a complete irrelevance. The response is amusing but relies on rhetoric rather than coherent argument and it is therefore ineffective in countering Street-Porter's.

Now try assessing this extract from an independently written article on obesity as if it were a response to Street-Porter. Imagine that you were faced with the following question, worth 10 marks:

> How effectively does the response by Gard counter Street-Porter's argument?
>
> *(10 marks)*

We should never lose sight of the fact that Western populations are, by and large, as healthy as they have ever been. We might also remember that there is a large body of opinion to the effect that one of the greatest threats to Western economic prosperity is our ageing population. While there are some that say we are about to see life expectancies nose dive, the majority of demographic opinion sees life expectancy continuing to rise. It is impossible for both points of view to be correct.

These complexities should direct us towards a focus on people's health and the quality of their lives as opposed to their body weight. Rather than making policies and laws that indiscriminately target everyone, we should be identifying those groups for whom access to physical activity and high-quality food is a problem. We know that people will use the streets for exercise if they think they are safe. We know that people who are poor and working multiple low-paid jobs will use junk food because it is cheap and convenient.

There is no all-encompassing obesity crisis but there are always areas of public health which are worthy of concerted attention. The past tells us that, if preventative public health is to be our goal, focussing on the material conditions of people's lives rather than hectoring, blaming and shaming them is more likely to achieve results.

(Extract from *Obesity and Public Policy: Thinking Clearly and Treading Carefully* by Dr Michael Gard, Charles Sturt University)

This task is more demanding than simply evaluating the reasoning in a passage as you need to consider it in relation to another argument. Begin the task by underlining the parts of Gard's argument that appear either to contradict or to confirm points made by Street-Porter.

We should never lose sight of the fact that <u>Western populations are, by and large, as healthy as they have ever been</u>. We might also remember that there is a large body of opinion to the effect that one of the greatest threats to Western economic prosperity is our ageing population. <u>While there are some that say we are about to see life expectancies nose dive, the majority of demographic opinion sees life expectancy continuing to rise.</u> It is impossible for both points of view to be correct.

These complexities should direct us towards a <u>focus on people's health and the quality of their lives as opposed to their body weight.</u> Rather than making <u>policies and laws that indiscriminately target everyone, we should be identifying those groups for whom access to physical activity and high-quality food is a problem</u>. We know that people will use the streets for exercise if they think they are safe. We know that people who are poor and working multiple low-paid jobs will use junk food because it is cheap and convenient.

<u>There is no all-encompassing obesity crisis</u> but there are always areas of public health which are worthy of concerted attention. The past tells us that, if preventative public health is to be our goal<u>, focussing on the material conditions of people's lives rather than hectoring, blaming and shaming them is more likely to achieve results</u>.

In the case of this short passage, most of it connects closely with points made by Street-Porter, but in a longer argument there might be strands about other issues. Underlining the relevant ones helps to focus your mind for comparison purposes.

The next step is to work your way through the underlined sections, identifying the extent to which they counter or confirm Street-Porter's claims and assessing whether Gard's reasoning is more or less effective than Street-Porter's. The focus of the question should of course be on Gard's reasoning; it would be inappropriate to return to detailed criticisms of Street-Porter. Here is a very thorough specimen answer:

> Gard begins with a direct contradiction of the claim made in Street-Porter's first two paragraphs, that 'Western populations are, by and large, as healthy as they have ever been'. Unlike Street-Porter he provides no immediate evidence for this specific claim, but the language he uses is moderate ('by and large') and academic, in contrast to the emotional appeals to the popular reader used by Street-Porter. This, together with his title, university background and the scholarly title of his article, gives an impression of expertise.

Gard moves on to acknowledge the counter-argument ('While there are some that say we are about to see life expectancies nose dive'), creating the impression of objectivity, before referring to what appears to be his own view, supported by 'the majority of demographic opinion'. Thus he shows that his view is corroborated by most experts. He also makes his case persuasive by using classical logic, the law of excluded middle, demonstrating that two contradictory statements cannot both be correct and thus leading the reader to accept his view that there is little danger of life expectancy being drastically reduced (as a result of people being overweight).

His acknowledgement of the 'complexities' in the situation is more reasonable and convincing than Street-Porter's suggestion that 'what we need is dead simple'. He counters her suggestions that body weight is highly significant by claiming that we should 'focus on people's health and the quality of their lives as opposed to their body weight'. This would be more convincing if he had provided a reason why healthy people's weight might have increased over time, giving examples such as bigger muscles due to greater access to gyms. Without this, he fails to address directly the concerns raised by the statistics in Street-Porter's article, despite assuring us that life expectancies have not decreased.

He objects to 'policies and laws that indiscriminately target everyone', thereby countering the rationing solution. His implication is that being overweight affects only certain groups ('There is no all-encompassing obesity crisis') and so targeted action would be better. As Street-Porter failed to demonstrate that 'all classes and income levels' are affected, this is quite credible. He supports this point by giving two examples illustrating why particular groups of people, those living in unsafe areas and the poorly paid, are more likely to be overweight, reinforcing this with the rhetorical device of repetition 'We know'. Though not backed by evidence, his points are reasonable and persuasive.

His concluding paragraph blends objective balance ('there are always areas of public health which are worthy of concerted attention') with an appeal to the reader's emotions in the form of a tricolon 'hectoring, blaming and shaming'.

Overall this is an effective challenge to Street-Porter's argument. Gard supports his points more logically, without any of the generalisations, assumptions and other flaws that undermine Street-Porter's. There are points where more evidence would help to support his case, but the greater willingness to acknowledge other viewpoints and complexities makes his argument generally more convincing.

Again this response is fuller than you could be expected to write in about 15 minutes but has been provided to demonstrate the types of assessment you could make. The descriptors for top-level marks in previous OCR questions of this type are along the following lines:

Criteria for top-level marks
- Candidates demonstrate sound, thorough and perceptive evaluation of strengths and weaknesses in Gard's response to Street-Porter's argument.
- They provide a consistent and accomplished evaluation of the extent to which Gard has supported his claims, and the extent to which these claims are an effective response to her argument.

- Candidates select key points to evaluate.
- Inappropriate forms of evaluation are rare and not serious.

This should be a reminder that for this type of question you need to strike a balance between thoroughness and exceeding your time limit. In other words, you should select the points that have the most significant bearing on your overall assessment, choosing a range of varied remarks that illustrate your knowledge of different types of strengths, flaws and rhetorical devices. Always remember that as well as making specific points of evaluation, you need to assess the overall effectiveness of the argument, in this case considering whether it is an effective challenge to Street-Porter's argument. In a longish essay like this, it is wise to write your overall assessment as a separate paragraph so that it is totally clear to the examiner that you have done this.

C Writing your own argument

Writing your own argument at A2 is more demanding than at AS, so you need to get plenty of practice and feedback from your teacher. The topics set for Unit 4 arguments tend to be more abstract than at AS, though it is still likely that you will be provided with a statement to support or challenge. Examinations in this unit for the previous specification asked candidates to write arguments supporting or challenging the following claims:

> Sometimes the right to argue has to be extended to the right to act.
>
> Freedom is meaningless without safety.
>
> Technological change should be welcomed.
>
> Equality is an unattainable dream.

It is highly likely that similar topics will be set in the new specification. The issues above are similar to those you will have encountered when discussing ethical dilemmas in Unit 3 and you should bring similar skills to bear, considering the complexity and ambiguity of terms such as 'freedom', 'technological change' and 'equality'. Your argument could include an attempt to define a key term and you might qualify your conclusion depending on how the term is interpreted.

Some of the reasons you include could be based on ethical positions such as utilitarianism or moral principles, and you could cite an alternative ethical position as a counterargument. This would be likely to result in a sophisticated answer and demonstrate a sound synoptic understanding of the whole course. (Nevertheless there is no requirement to mention ethical positions.)

You will need to spend some time thinking widely about the issue, as you will not be credited for repetition of any of the arguments or evidence in the passage. For example, the passage in the previous specification accompanying the essay title 'Equality is an unattainable dream' was entirely about feminism but the question invites more of an overview. It is unlikely that a candidate whose argument focused exclusively on feminism would score as well as one who included examples and evidence about other equality

C Writing your own argument

issues, such as class, race and disability, though there would be no harm in making some references to feminism that were very different from those in the passage. A sophisticated candidate might differentiate between equality of access or opportunity, at least in the eyes of the law, and fully realised equality of achievement, which is much harder to obtain.

Thus it is important to consider both the content of your argument and its structure.

Assessment Objective 3 at A2 requires you to:

> Develop and communicate relevant and coherent arguments clearly and accurately in a concise and logical manner.

Your argument should have the following characteristics:

- The argument must be a response to the precise title set, not a slightly different topic, and the title must make it clear whether the argument is intended to support or challenge the statement.
- The argument's structure should be complex compared with AS. Include several strands of reasoning supporting a number of intermediate conclusions. There should be several reasons in each strand, most of them supported by examples and evidence.
- Use of analogies, sustained hypothetical reasoning and principles is rewarded where appropriate.
- Despite its complexity, the argument must be coherent. The points must be logically grouped so the argument flows. It is essential that the conclusion is clearly stated and well supported by all the reasoning. Prior planning is essential.
- The argument must be persuasive. This means selecting appropriate issues you are reasonably informed about and ensuring that your reasons are relevant and adequate, not making exaggerated claims of the sort you may have encountered in slippery slope arguments. Evidence and examples must be convincing, avoiding references to imaginary research. Your argument will not qualify for top-band marks if unreasonable assumptions have to be made.
- Where appropriate, recognise contrasting points of view and identify the reasoning underpinning those points of view, identifying and evaluating clearly and precisely the arguments on either side. This means you should include counter-arguments in preference to counter-claims, as it is necessary to identify the reasons behind these claims before you can challenge them effectively with a thorough response. There might be scope for treating more than one counter-argument in this way.
- Allow plenty of thinking time and prioritise quality over quantity. A carefully organised, convincing and sophisticated argument of 300 words is likely to be more highly rewarded than a rambling argument of twice the length. A recent OCR marking scheme commented, 'Candidates will not have time to produce thorough arguments covering all possible strands of reasoning and responding to all counter-arguments. We should reward candidates who have demonstrated the ability to argue cogently, coherently and concisely. We are looking for an intelligent, thoughtful, structured response.'
- Your language must be 'capable of dealing with complexity', so write in a formal register using mature vocabulary. Check your work for errors of spelling, grammar and punctuation, as these aspects of communication are assessed. OCR's guidelines on quality of language include the following: 'We want to credit language which means something and which is clear, succinct and precise. We want to credit commu-

nication of good thinking. We do not want to over-reward flowery or waffly language which says very little.'

Consider the argument below, trying to identify respects in which it meets the requirements listed above. It is a response to a question arising from the Janet Street-Porter passage.

'Look where free choice has got us'. Write your own argument to support or challenge the view that allowing the public free choice of lifestyle is harmful.

(20 marks)

An argument supporting the conclusion that giving the public free choice of lifestyle is harmful

It has become fashionable to criticise the 'nanny state', arguing that it is unnecessary to tell members of the public how to live their lives, but this view is misguided.

Libertarians give the impression that allowing personal choice of lifestyle for the individual is paramount, but this takes no account of the fact that in a modern community, individual choices have public implications. If individuals choose to indulge in unhealthy practices, such as smoking, drug taking or over-indulgence in fattening foods and alcohol, then the public, through the increase costs of their care to the National Health Service, will be adversely affected. Thus freedom for the individual to pursue an unhealthy lifestyle can mean less freedom for tax payers who could otherwise spend their earnings in other ways.

Libertarians may counter this by suggesting that the welfare state be dispensed with so that we need no longer be burdened with the cost to the NHS of those who opt to take risks with their health. This is an inhumane suggestion, removing essential care from those who are sick or needy through no fault of their own. Moreover, others would still be affected by the folly of individuals allowed by a careless state to make unhealthy choices. Their friends and relatives would be saddened by their illnesses and their dependants would be let down by their reduced earning power. The economy and society as a whole would be unable to benefit from the contribution these people would otherwise have made. To pursue unhealthy choices is therefore selfish and should be discouraged.

A further factor to consider is public ignorance. Ordinary people are not in a position to know about the latest research into the possible effects of particular substances unless informed by reliable sources such as government campaigns. Young people will continue to view cannabis smoking as relatively harmless and risk mental breakdown unless warnings are issued and laws enforced. Very young people and the semi-literate are particularly at risk. Healthcare is a human right and it is a violation of that right to deny information and protection to vulnerable groups so a paternalist approach is more ethical than a libertarian one.

We do not release tigers from their cages in zoos to allow children the option of stroking the animals. Neither do we allow motorists to drive on whichever side of the road they like. In such cases the risks, to the individuals concerned or the public as a whole, outweigh the benefits of choice. Governments have a duty to do whatever is best for the majority. Giving the public free choice of lifestyle is harmful.

C Writing your own argument

You should have been able to identify that this argument fulfils most of the requirements listed above.

- Each paragraph is a short argument in its own right; in other words a strand in the longer argument.
- The final sentence of each paragraph except for the last ends in an intermediate conclusion.
- The first two paragraphs begin with counter-arguments, which are then challenged.
- There are plenty of relevant reasons, supported by examples of harmful behaviours such as cannabis smoking.
- The argument refers to libertarianism, paternalism and human rights, showing the candidate can use material from Unit 3, reflecting the synoptic nature of this unit.
- The argument includes hypothetical reasoning (paragraph 2), a principle in the penultimate paragraph and two analogies in the final one, displaying the ability to employ a variety of components.

Can you detect any weaknesses in the argument? The analogy about the uncaged tigers is rather far-fetched, making the argument a little less convincing at that point, but I think you will agree that the content is otherwise reasonable and this candidate's argument should be placed in the top level.

Bearing the time limit in mind, she could have dispensed with the first part of her final paragraph and probably still scored just as well. Remember that OCR are looking for 'an intelligent, thoughtful, structured response' rather than 'thorough arguments covering all possible strands of reasoning'.

The OCR descriptors for the top level for writing your own argument to support or challenge a claim (worth 16–20 marks) are as follows:

Criteria for top-level marks
- Candidates produce cogent, sound and perceptive reasoning using clear strands of reasoning. Reasons and intermediate conclusions give strong support to conclusion and argument structure is accomplished, possibly complex. Blips rare.
- Language clear, precise and capable of dealing with complexity.
- Candidates anticipate and respond effectively to key counter-arguments.
- Grammar, spelling and punctuation are very good. Errors are few, if any.

D Revision checklist for Unit 4

1 The examination

OCR codes
- A2 Critical Thinking subject code: H452
- Unit 4 code: F504

Mark allocation

60 marks, 25% of the total Advanced GCE marks. The paper may not be divided into sections as such but questions in the specimen paper were grouped under the headings 'Analyse', 'Evaluate' and 'Develop your own reasoning'. Answer all questions, some of which will require short answers and some essays.

This is a synoptic paper as it tests the skills you developed during AS (AO1, AO2 and AO3) and you may, in writing your own argument, be able to refer to ethical theories learnt in Unit 3. This means you must carefully revise all material from the other three units as well as the new material in this unit. Quality of written communication is assessed under AO3.

Timing

1 hour 30 minutes. Take care to reserve plenty of time for the argument of your own.

Practicalities

Unlike the AS papers, there will be no ruled spaces on the question paper for your answers. You will need to write in the general type of answer book used for most examinations in black ink. As this gives you no guidance on how much to write for particular questions, time yourself when you do practice papers to see what you can realistically achieve. How you divide your time between essays analysing and assessing the passage and writing the argument of your own needs to relate closely to the number of marks allocated to each.

2 The requirements of Unit 4

This question paper consists of complex materials in the form of one or more passages (maximum 1,250 words). They could include images, statistics, diagrams etc. for analysis and evaluation. Questions will require short or more discursive answers.

Unit 4 resembles Unit 2 in the skills required, but it needs a greater level of sophistication and some additional knowledge. (It differs in that Unit 4 has no multiple-choice questions.) It is similar in that you are required to:

- analyse parts of a passage and identify its components (AO1)
- evaluate parts of the argument, identifying weaknesses and strengths (AO2)
- write your own argument in response to the passage (AO3)

Important differences are outlined below.

3 Analysis

- The passage is likely to be a genuine article from the media, written for an educated audience.
- It will not be a simply structured argument but one with several developed strands of reasoning. There may be other elements, some of which you may need to identify by name and critically analyse, such as:
  - scene setting
  - explanation
  - clarification
  - rhetorical devices

– rant
– questions
– repetition

- There are likely to be several low-marks questions quoting phrases from the passage and asking you to identify and briefly explain their function in the passage. For example, as well as stating that a particular sentence was an intermediate conclusion, you might say that it was supported by the three reasons in the preceding paragraph.

- You may be asked to analyse the structure of a whole paragraph or strand of reasoning in detail. You can make use of diagrams and recognised notations to clarify this but would be expected to answer in sentences too as the question could be worth about 12 marks.

- You should refer to the need for specific assumptions at appropriate points of the argument, even though these are not a visible part of it.

- As well as recognising the basic elements of argument studied in Units 1 and 2, you will be expected to be able to recognise and explain the function of the following:
  – joint or independent reasons
  – multiple intermediate conclusions
  – developed counter-arguments
  – analogies
  – suppositional or hypothetical reasoning
  – principles

4 Evaluation

- Any flaws in the passage will not have been deliberately inserted by examiners, so they may be harder to identify than those you encountered in Units 1 and 2.

- Instead of being directed to assess flaws or elements such as analogies in specific paragraphs for a couple of marks, you may be expected to evaluate the support given to a claim over several paragraphs. This will require an essay worth about 10 marks, considering the strengths and weaknesses of the reasoning in a developed strand of the argument. The relevance and adequacy of any diagrams, images, examples or statistics used in support of the argument may have to be considered.

- Unlike at AS, having identified specific strengths and weaknesses, you should offer a general conclusion about how well overall this particular strand of the argument supports the claim being made. You might suggest an alternative conclusion that could be drawn from the reasoning.

- As well as identifying the types of weaknesses and strengths studied in Units 1 and 2, including making use of credibility criteria, you should be able to recognise the following and comment on their effects on the reasoning:
  – deductively valid argument structures such as affirming the antecedent (modus ponens) and denying the consequent (modus tollens)
  – formal fallacies, affirming the consequent and denying the antecedent
  – syllogisms
  – fallacy of the undistributed middle
  – false converse
  – appeals
  – other rhetorical devices such as rhetorical questions and parallelism

- More detailed assessment of analogies and hypothetical reasoning may be needed.
- Any assumptions will need to be identified and assessed.
- You may be asked to evaluate moves from one strand of the argument to another in a short essay worth about 10 marks. For example, the writer may make a claim in one part of the argument and then introduce a case study which seems only marginally relevant, or perhaps reach a conclusion which seems inconsistent with some of the material in the passage. This requires you to take a holistic overview of the passage, assessing its development through the various strands to its conclusion, which was not expected at AS.

5 *Writing your own argument*

- Developing your own reasoning will be more challenging as the topic suggested is likely to be more abstract than in Unit 2. The specimen paper invites candidates to support or challenge the claim that 'Freedom is meaningless without safety'. This reflects the subject of the passage, which is about crime and levels of policing and surveillance, but a good argument might incorporate examples from other fields.
- As Unit 4 is a synoptic paper, you are likely to benefit from your Unit 3 experience of thinking carefully about the ambiguity of language, identifying principles and ethical dilemmas when selecting material for your own argument.
- Your argument needs to be longer and have a more complex structure than at AS. Several strands of reasoning are expected, with argument and counter-argument and several intermediate conclusions. Examples and evidence must be persuasive with only a few reasonable assumptions being required. Additional elements such as analogies and sustained hypothetical reasoning are welcomed.

From 2008, exceptionally high attainment at A-level will be recognised by a new grading system. Candidates achieving at least 320 UMS marks in their Advanced GCE, i.e. grade A, who also gain at least 180 UMS in their two A2 units, will receive an A* grade.

Key terms index

Key terms index